THE
BLOOD

═══ REVISED EDITION ═══

THE
BLOOD

— REVISED EDITION —

BENNY HINN

CHARISMA
HOUSE

Cataloging-in-Publication Data is on file with the Library of Congress.
International Standard Book Number: 978-1-63641-355-6
E-book ISBN: 978-1-63641-356-3

1 2024
Printed in the United States of America

Most Charisma Media products are available at special quantity discounts for bulk purchase for sales promotions, premiums, fund-raising, and educational needs. For details, call us at (407) 333-0600 or visit our website at www.charismamedia.com.

The revised edition of this book could not have been compiled without the help of some good friends: Stephen Strang and the staff at Charisma House and Charisma Media, Neil Eskelin, Dr. J. Rodman Williams, Dudley Hall, my coworkers at Benny Hinn Ministries, and so many others. Thank you.

CONTENTS

FOREWORD

THE LAST THING I'm likely to do on vacation is watch a Christian telecast. I'm a broadcaster myself, so tuning in to TV while I'm on vacation is anything but a change of pace. It was unusual, then, that I paused to watch anything, especially a Benny Hinn broadcast, since I'd never really taken the time to watch one before. That event is a very special memory to me now.

I had no idea what God was about to do in my heart when I stopped "paging" with the TV remote and began noticing with a sense of gratitude the beauty of the worship taking place on Benny Hinn's program.

Benny has so many who love his ministry that it's a bit risky even to suggest I ever had any different impression of him. It can smack of criticism, professional jealousy, or just plain unkindness. But I had never felt any of those things, nor did I ever stand opposed to Benny Hinn.

I simply had been busy with my own responsibilities and had no time for either (1) becoming more aware of his ministry or (2) being concerned with those who did criticize him. In short, I had no relationship with the man and no feelings, either positive or negative, about him.

Except for one.

I did feel that the little I'd seen and heard indicated that God's hand was on him, even though at times I was puzzled by his style—by the distracting practices I noted when paging by a telecast en route to something else. But now I was watching.

As I observed the precious spirit of worship, I leaned back in my chair in the mountain cabin where my wife, Anna, and I were vacationing and began to enter into the praise that was wafting heavenward. Jesus was the center of attention. The name of Jesus was being magnificently glorified and adored. And as Benny led the service, I thought, "This man is an instrument in the hands of the Holy Spirit to bring people into the presence of God."

I'd never seen him lead others in worshipping Jesus, but as I watched, something happened: God placed a distinct brotherly love for him in my heart. It was so pointedly and so clearly an action of the Father in my soul that I later thought about Mark's words describing Jesus when the inquiring young man came to Him: "Then Jesus, looking at him, loved him" (Mark 10:21).

Benny and I had met once, briefly, when he and his wife greeted me in a restaurant in Birmingham, England, where we each were speaking locally. But there was no way to suggest we had any real acquaintance.

Then suddenly, at this moment in the middle of my vacation, I knew God had given me a special sense of kinship with a man I hardly knew—in fact, one who more than anyone else I knew was often under criticism, though I was neither a foe nor in any personal way a friend. But right then, on that day, I "loved" the man with a heart full of gratitude to the God whose love often overflows our hearts by surprise.

It's interesting to look back on such moments—those times we all experience when the Holy Spirit is "up to something" but we have no idea what it is.

That's the way I view that summertime moment several years ago. There was no way I could know then that within a very few weeks my telephone would ring and I'd be conversing with Benny Hinn for the first time.

It's for Benny himself to tell the details sometime of how God led him to contact a small number of leaders—most of whom knew him no better than I did—and ask for their counsel. I admired and commended him for doing this, not because I was one of those he trusted enough to ask counsel of, but because I know of nothing more important for spiritual leaders to do than to submit themselves to one another.

To do so is not to substitute human counsel for Holy Spirit

direction. It is wise to acknowledge the facts of our humanness and our vulnerability to independent attitudes. It is those attitudes that open the door to the potential we all have for confusion, failure, error, or lack of wisdom in how we serve in our personal callings.

"Brother Hayford," he said, "God is blessing my ministry in ways I could never imagine and could never produce. What is happening to me is something that I know He is doing, and I feel the need of brethren to whom I can turn and ask for input. We've all seen ministries fail for lack of accountability, and I don't want to be an embarrassment to the body of Christ. Would you be willing to let me come and spend time talking with you about God's ways and God's work?"

Even while he was speaking, I knew why the Holy Spirit had prompted my heart those few days before. As we conversed, I expressed my friendly availability—"Benny, God's hand is on you to bring people into His presence. I'll be glad to do anything I can to help you keep your ministry focused so that people are aware of Jesus more than of you, because I believe that's what you really want."

Since that time, Benny Hinn has testified to his desire to renew his focus on the essentials of the truth of God's Word in his ministry and to remove anything that would distract from his priority: to glorify Jesus Christ alone, our loving and mighty Savior.

Hosts of leaders like me are confirming this assertive effort on the part of a God-graced messenger to be what he is called to be. Praise God for the Christlike humility that is, I believe, opening the door to a vastly broadened ministry of Jesus' life and power through a vessel named Benny.

This book is one of the hallmarks of this new time in his life. It is not only a pointed focus on the ultimate foundational essential in the gospel, but it is also a fresh, Spirit-anointed truth to which I believe He—the Holy Spirit—is seeking to alert all God's people at this time.

Only days before Benny Hinn invited me to write this foreword, I had experienced a very special heart-stirring concerning the blood of Jesus. So profound was the quickening that I had set aside time for study and made plans to bring a series on this subject to my flock at The Church On The Way.

Discovering the plans for this book deepened my conviction: *the blood of Jesus is a primary theme the Holy Spirit has for the church today.*

Why? First, all power that flows to mankind with redeeming grace and glory flows because of the blood of Jesus. Second, no confusion about the Savior's person or work can abide in an atmosphere where the blood and the cross are taught in the light of God's Word. And third, *no power of hell* can withstand the proclamation of the blood of Jesus, whether it is declared from a pulpit or spoken over a home or a heart.

I'm grateful that this book has been written. It is a testimony to the greatest truth known to mankind: that the Son of God has declared, "It is finished," and that through His blood and cross *alone*, He has broken the power of sin, death, and hell. He is the Lord!

It is also a testimony of a man's answer to God's call to focus on priorities that will point every listener, viewer, or reader to Jesus—and bring them into the presence of God. Glory to the Lamb that was slain!

—JACK W. HAYFORD
FOUNDING PASTOR, THE CHURCH ON THE WAY
FORMER CHANCELLOR, THE KING'S COLLEGE AND SEMINARY
VAN NUYS, CALIFORNIA

THERE'S POWER
in the BLOOD

ONE OF THE highlights of the year in my opinion is our annual Good Friday service, one that I always look forward to with great anticipation. Each year we select a different city in which to hold a Candlelight Communion Miracle Service.

Volunteer workers spend hours preparing for the service. In addition to the normal setup, they prepare thousands of individually packaged little glasses of grape juice and wafers, symbols of the body and the blood of Jesus Christ, to be used in the Communion service. These items have been placed at hundreds of key locations throughout the arena so that the ushers can easily distribute them at the appropriate time in the service. People travel from many cities, states, and even other countries by the thousands to share these precious moments together in the presence of the Savior.

The glory of God and the presence of Holy Spirit fill the arena, which is jammed to capacity. There's also an overflow crowd of thousands in an adjacent auditorium. As the service begins, thousands of voices proclaim the power of Christ's blood in song: "There's power, power, wonder-working power in the precious blood of the Lamb."[1]

The lights dim slightly as the ushers begin to light the candles on the platform while soft worship music continues: "O the blood of Jesus, it washes white as snow."[2]

In moments a hushed quiet descends upon the massive crowd as the anointing of the Holy Spirit descends upon expectant hearts. The penitent worshippers who have gathered for this service are deeply stirred as the rich, powerful sense of God's presence fills every heart to overflowing with a passion and love for Jesus Christ. With genuine adoration, hungry hearts are called by the lyrics of the song being sung: "Precious Lamb of glory..."[3]

The ushers begin to distribute the Communion elements row by row. As each individual receives the container holding the little glass of grape juice and the wafer, he stands in reverence, waiting to participate in this special Communion service with the thousands who have assembled.

> For I received from the Lord that which I also delivered to you: that the Lord Jesus on the same night in which He was betrayed took bread; and when He had given thanks, He broke it and said, "Take, eat; this is My body which is broken for you; do this in remembrance of Me." In the same manner He also took the cup after supper, saying, "This cup is the new covenant in My blood. This do, as often as you drink it, in remembrance of Me." For as often as you eat this bread and drink this cup, you proclaim the Lord's death till He comes.
> —1 CORINTHIANS 11:23–26

Almost immediately the miracles begin to take place all over the coliseum. The applause of the crowd echoes throughout the arena as deaf ears are opened, wheelchairs are emptied, the crippled and lame walk, and blind eyes see. It's a glorious celebration of God's power.

Years ago I discovered that where the blood is honored, the presence of God descends and miracles take place. As we remember the work of the cross and recognize the power represented in the shed blood of Jesus, lives are touched and transformed by God's presence and power.

Our loving heavenly Father has been so faithful year after year, and we've been so blessed as we've worshipped in the powerful, precious, holy presence of the Holy Spirit and witnessed His matchless power.

It's because we've experienced that power in such mighty ways over and over again that I feel compelled to share with you a revelation of the blood of Jesus that I received many years ago.

The power of Christ's blood is not limited to a particular ministry or outreach. As you will discover throughout the following pages, the blood of Jesus Christ and the power associated with it are available to you and your loved ones. The most important revelation of the blood of Jesus Christ is that its power to save, heal, and cleanse is for you!

Get ready to discover and experience the wonderful and mighty power of *The Blood*.

—BENNY HINN

PART I

THE BLESSINGS OF THE BLOOD COVENANT

Iɴ Pᴀʀᴛ I, our focus will be upon what it means to enter into blood covenant and the significance of God's blood covenant with us. We will discover the benefits of keeping this covenant, such as salvation, cleansing, protection, and security.

As you begin your study of *The Blood*, read the material carefully and thoroughly. At the end of each chapter, beginning with chapter 2, you will find an interactive study section titled "A Covenant to Keep." This study section is based upon the chapter's material and is included to help you gain a deeper understanding about God's blood covenant with you. It's important to read every Scripture passage. As you read the scriptures and complete the study questions at the end of each chapter, pray and ask the Holy Spirit for wisdom, understanding, and insight. Apply what you learn about the blood to your daily walk in the Spirit.

Chapter 1

POWER and PROMISE

ISRAEL IS A unique and wonderful land. For the first sixteen years of my life it was all I knew, for it was in Jaffa, Israel, that I was born and spent most of my childhood.

Although the majority of Jaffa's citizens were Jewish, my family was not. My mother, Clemence, was of Armenian descent. And my father, Costandi, came from a family that had emigrated from Greece to Egypt and then to Palestine. To add to my multicultural childhood, I was christened in the Greek Orthodox Church, and I spoke French at the school I attended, Arabic in our home, and Hebrew in the community.

I believe that being raised in Israel has given me a deep appreciation and respect for the people of that land. Because of their history, the Jewish people have a deep emotional bond to their land that is beyond description, one that continually draws them back to their homeland. For centuries traditions have been passed down from generation to generation, and many of these customs and traditions are still observed today.

The familiar streets of Jaffa and the beautiful turquoise waters of the Mediterranean that embrace the rocky shoreline of this coastal city are forever etched in my memory. I can still remember the warmth of the afternoon sun caressing my face as I walked home from school day after day. The familiar sounds and smells in the streets as I walked along were always there to remind me that home was just up the hill.

For me each day was predictable and basically like the next, even though the threat of war was always a possibility. I can vaguely remember my parents discussing it at times. But I didn't feel personally threatened—that is, until the Six-Day War in 1967.

Immediately after those six long, terrifying days of war and conflict, my father gathered our family together and announced that we would be emigrating to another country. The following year we left everything that was familiar to us and headed for Toronto, Canada: the place that was to become our new home. We arrived there with just a few earthly possessions and the bare necessities. At age sixteen, I suddenly found myself in a new country where the culture, climate, and language were different. The changes meant a new school, new acquaintances, and even new and different clothing, for I was suddenly forced to cope with cold and snow for months on end. Then there were new holidays and new traditions. Everything was different except my family!

Initially, all these changes were very traumatic for me, and I had a difficult time making the transition to my new surroundings. But in 1972 my life was totally transformed by an encounter with Jesus Christ at a morning prayer meeting conducted by some of the students at the school I attended. What I experienced that morning at ten minutes to eight was glorious, and I have never been the same since.

At home after school I found a big black Bible that had not been used for years. I read from the Gospels nonstop for hours, and as my eyes pored over the pages of this sacred book, I found myself saying out loud, "Jesus, come into my heart." As indescribable peace and joy flooded my being, I knew beyond any doubt that my prayer had been answered.

Later that same week I joined my newly found Christian friends in attending their church. The people who attended there were an exuberant throng of Christians who met every Thursday in St. Paul's Cathedral, an Anglican church located in downtown Toronto.

It didn't take long for me to realize that this group of people was different from any other group I had ever encountered. Although I was born and raised in Israel and had grown up surrounded by the historic sites found in Scripture, I quickly discovered that they understood a great deal about the land of my birth. And the songs they sang and the prayers I heard them pray spoke openly about the blood of Christ. This was something totally new to me. They would sing, "O the blood of Jesus!" And they would pray, "Lord, cover us with Your blood." They spoke these words with power and authority.

If you have read my book *Good Morning, Holy Spirit*, you know what happened to me just before Christmas in 1973 when I had a personal encounter with the Holy Spirit. My life was totally transformed, and from that moment on the Bible took on a whole new dimension for me. Day after day I spent hours in prayer and the study of God's Word. I became absorbed in Scripture, and the Holy Spirit became my friend and guide.

I was like a thirsty sponge as I studied and learned about everything from the story of creation to the marriage supper of the Lamb. As I read from the pages of God's Word, many of the truths I learned had special meaning to me; I recognized many of the sites mentioned in Scripture, for I had visited them on many occasions while living in Israel. And what I didn't understand, I asked the Holy Spirit to open my understanding and reveal to me.

As I pored over the pages of my Bible, studying and praying while taking in each word, I realized that God's relationship to man was held together by a blood covenant. Over and over I saw this principle repeated in the Word of God, and as I contemplated this I recalled my experience a year earlier when I had heard my friends sing about the blood of Jesus and pray, "Lord, cover us with Your blood." I began to understand the power connected with the blood of Jesus, and I longed to know more.

DAYS OF DISCOVERY

During those exciting days as a young Christian, I was attending a church on Sundays pastored by Maxwell Whyte. He was an outstanding teacher of God's Word who became a spiritual mentor to me. Pastor Whyte was the minister who baptized me in water.

One of his constant themes was the blood of Christ. His accounts of the outpouring of the Holy Spirit at the turn of the century will never be erased from my memory. He told the story of the mighty move of the Holy Spirit that came to Kilsyth, Scotland, in 1908. Pastor Whyte said that the visitation came spontaneously as a result of recognizing the power of the blood of Jesus. He said, "A brother named John Reid, sitting in the midst of the prayer group, suddenly raised his hands and said, 'The blood of Jesus.'"

Immediately the Holy Spirit descended on the gathering, and people began to receive the Pentecostal experience all over the room. The revival spread throughout England.[1]

In his book *The Power of the Blood*, Pastor Whyte tells of living in England during World War II.

> We went through many dangerous air raids when buzz bombs were flying everywhere. But we were able to lie down with our children and sleep through much of it. The protection of the Blood of Jesus was so real that it seemed like we were sleeping in a strong shelter. In fact, we used to speak of the Blood as the "best air raid shelter in the world."[2]

Pastor Whyte said that every night before they went to sleep they would ask the Lord to cover them, their home, and their children with the blood. One night thirteen bombs landed within three-quarters of a mile from their home. Aside from some minor damage to the house, they were all kept safe.

I remember Pastor Whyte telling our congregation again and again, "I have never known the active, audible pleading of the blood to fail."

Because of his ministry, my interest in the power of the blood of Christ grew and multiplied. I began to study it for myself to see what the Word really said.

HE GAVE HIS LIFE

Many years later, after I became a pastor, God gave me an understanding of the blood covenant that would forever change my life and ministry.

One Saturday afternoon I had stayed home to study the Scriptures about the blood covenant so I could teach it to my congregation. I was sitting outside in the backyard of my home studying and praying. "Lord, give me an understanding of the blood," I asked. The second I said that, I felt the presence of the Lord and began to weep.

That day the blood of Christ took on a whole new meaning. The Holy Spirit began showing me that the blood of Jesus represents His life. I realized more than ever that when Christ shed His blood at Calvary, He gave us His very life. And when we ask the Lord to wash us and cover us with His blood, we will experience His life-giving power.

Throughout my ministry I have seen that Christians have a limited knowledge of the atonement. As a result, they have not experienced the freedom God has for their lives.

For example, many believers tell me that Satan continues to oppress and harass them. It comes as a surprise when I tell them I have not experienced any demonic oppression on my life since I began asking God in prayer to cover me with the blood.

Before that I was depressed at times and felt that my mind was blocked. Sometimes when I prayed, I felt a horrible oppression come upon me. Occasionally, I had nightmares and at times felt that something was literally choking me.

But when God gave me that enormous understanding of the blood and I began to ask for a blood covering in prayer, that "thing" was completely broken. Years have passed since I have had that kind of attack, and I am grateful for the liberty I have experienced because of that understanding.

There is power in the blood of Jesus. There is no question about it. Yet at the same time, the blood does not have "magical" power. The power comes from the Lord Jesus Himself, and He is the One who will act on your behalf when you appropriate the power represented by His shed blood as you apply the blood through prayer.

We apply Jesus' blood through prayer and faith. But it is the Lord who covers us; we do not cover ourselves. Why have I written this book?

- To open your eyes to the importance God places on the topic of the blood covenant

- To demonstrate the power of the blood of Jesus

- To show how you and I can come into God's presence through the blood of His Son

- To help you understand the great grace that God bestows on us because of the blood of Jesus

- To lead you to a greater freedom in Christ than you have ever experienced

This is a book I want you to read with your Bible open. If God places such an emphasis on the blood from Genesis to Revelation, there is a message in His Word for you.

THE COMPLETED PICTURE

When I asked the Holy Spirit to give me an understanding of the blood covenant, I had dozens of questions. But He gave me the answers from the Word, and I want to share them with you.

- What does the Scripture mean in Hebrews 12:24 when it says that the blood "speaks better things than that of Abel"?

- Why was the leper sprinkled with blood seven times (Lev. 14:7)?

- How can the blood of Jesus be applied in our lives today?

- How is God's grace connected to the blood of His Son?

- How can the blood of Christ provide protection for your household?

- What does the Scripture teach about the blood of the cross and the anointing?

- What does Hebrews 9:12 mean when it says, "With His own blood He entered the Most Holy Place once for all, having obtained eternal redemption"?

- How can we use the blood of Jesus to defeat the enemy in our lives?

I pray that as you continue reading, you will gain a greater understanding of the blood covenant and experience God's wonderful presence.

Chapter 2

FROM the
BEGINNING

OUR HOME IN Jaffa seemed much larger than it was. To save land, the building was designed for three families, with a separate home on each level.

Mr. Hanna and his family lived on the top floor. He was a Lebanese gentleman who was married to a Jewish woman from Hungary. But Mr. Hanna was more than just a neighbor; he and my father had developed such a special bond that he became like a second father to the eight children in our family. As a result of that relationship, Mr. Hanna and my father made a commitment to one another in a very dramatic way.

Mr. Hanna and my father, Costandi, entered into a pact that will never be erased from my memory. Using a razor-sharp blade, both men made an incision on their wrists until blood seeped to the surface. Then they placed their wrists tightly together and allowed the blood to mingle.

On the table before them were two glasses of wine. My father held his wrist over one of the goblets and let several drops of blood fall into it. Mr. Hanna did the same with the second glass.

Next, they mixed the wine together, and each drank from the other man's cup. At that moment they became blood brothers. In the Eastern culture and among many other people of the world, it is the strongest bond that can be made between two men.

For this kind of covenant, some Easterners will also sign a written agreement that says, "If you are unable to provide for your children, I will become a father to them and sustain them. If you become ill or die, I will be responsible for the well-being of your family."

It is more than a legal pact. It is a vow that is sealed in blood and will never be broken.

When our family emigrated from Israel to Canada and I became a Christian, the Holy Spirit began to reveal God's Word to me. I had seen the influence of the blood pact in the Eastern culture from a natural perspective. Then, from a spiritual perspective, the Holy Spirit showed me how much more powerful God's blood covenant is. From Genesis to Revelation there is a crimson stream that is the life-giving source of power, protection, and promise for you and for me today.

THE BREATH OF LIFE

The story of creation itself marks the beginning of the role of the blood covenant in God's plan for humanity.

Our creation was a three-step process.

First, "the LORD God formed man of the dust of the ground" (Gen. 2:7). I can almost see Him scooping some mud into His hand and literally squeezing it into shape.

Second, God "breathed into his nostrils the breath of life" (Gen. 2:7). At this point, I believe our spirits came into being. The Scriptures often represent God's Spirit as His breath. So I believe God as a Spirit created our spirits.

Third, "man became a living soul" (Gen. 2:7, KJV). After man received his body and spirit, then he was a distinct individual (or a soul).

The spirit, body, and soul that God created have distinct functions.

- The *spirit* within us is the part that knows God intimately. It is God-conscious.

- Our *body* is the shell we dwell in. It is world-conscious.

- The *soul* is our intellect, will, and emotions. It is self-conscious.

11

Like an archaeologist unearthing a hidden treasure, I was jubilant as I studied the Word of God and realized the distinct parts God created. My spirit is the part of me that communes with God, my physical being is what is in contact with the earthly things of this world, and my soul is the part that feels, understands, thinks, and decides.

I believe another amazing thing occurred at creation. Leviticus records, "The life of the flesh is in the blood" (Lev. 17:11). Therefore, when God breathed the breath of life into Adam, I believe his blood was enlivened.

For centuries, medical science has studied the powerful functions of blood. They know it carries oxygen and food through our bodies by circulating through our veins and arteries. It also acts as a defense against infection. But there is much that they don't know about the importance God places on the blood.

CHAOS IN THE GARDEN

As we begin to comprehend the tremendous power of the blood covenant, it is important to recall what happened in the Garden of Eden. When God created Adam, he was a perfect being. He had a mind so magnificent that he was able to name every animal and remember the name of each kind.

At that time, the first man and woman lived in perfect harmony with God. He walked with them in the cool of the day. They had fellowship, and they knew God intimately.

But an enemy was lurking in the garden.

> Now the serpent was more cunning than any beast of the field which the LORD God had made. And he said to the woman, "Has God indeed said, 'You shall not eat of every tree of the garden'?"
>
> —GENESIS 3:1

Satan was cunning and sly. He came to the woman with a question about God's instructions regarding eating from the tree. He asked her, "Has God indeed said, 'You shall not eat of every tree of the garden'?" (Gen. 3:1).

The devil wields this weapon of words because he wants us to question God—His faithfulness, His love, His promises, and His power. He was questioning the woman: "Did God really say that?" Her response shows she believed the tempter rather than what God said because she disobeyed.

The woman replied to the serpent, "We may eat the fruit of the trees of the garden; but of the fruit of the tree which is in the midst of the garden, God has said, 'You shall not eat it, nor shall you touch it, *lest you die*'" (Gen. 3:2–3, emphasis added).

Eve only said, "...lest you die," but the Lord said, "You shall *surely* die" (Gen. 2:17, emphasis added).

Then Satan lied to the woman and said, "You will not surely die. For God knows that in the day you eat of it your eyes will be opened, and you will be like God, knowing good and evil" (Gen. 3:4–5).

It has always been Satan's desire to be like God. Scripture records that he said in his heart, "I will ascend into heaven, I will exalt my throne above the stars of God" (Isa. 14:13).

Satan had been banished from heaven for trying to be like God. There in the Garden of Eden he was attempting to offer the same promise of godlike status to the first woman. And he has not stopped. Thousands of years later, he is still planting the same thoughts into unsuspecting hearts.

THE FLESH AND THE DEVIL

The first woman not only fell for the lie, but she also gave the fruit to Adam, and he joined her.

> And when the woman saw that the tree was good for food, and that it was pleasant to the eyes, and a tree to be desired to

make one wise, she took of the fruit thereof, and did eat, and gave also unto her husband with her; and he did eat.

—GENESIS 3:6, KJV

In that one Scripture verse we find three great temptations Satan uses:

1. The lust of the flesh (The tree was good for food.)

2. The lust of the eyes (It was pleasant to look at.)

3. The pride of life (The tree offered wisdom.)

Why does the enemy bring these forms of temptation against us? His deadly design is to lure us into a sinful world. But we are warned:

Do not love the world or the things in the world. If anyone loves the world, the love of the Father is not in him. For all that is in the world—the lust of the flesh, the lust of the eyes, and the pride of life—is not of the Father but is of the world.

—1 JOHN 2:15–16

Satan tried the same three temptations during his encounter with Jesus in the desert. He said, "If You are the Son of God, command that these stones become bread" (Matt. 4:3). What was he offering? The lust of the flesh.

When "the devil took Him up on an exceedingly high mountain, and showed Him all the kingdoms of the world and their glory" (Matt. 4:8), he tempted Christ with the lust of the eyes. And he appealed to the pride of life by saying to the Lord:

If You are the Son of God, throw Yourself down. For it is written: "He shall give His angels charge over you," and, "In their hands they shall bear you up, lest you dash your foot against a stone."

—MATTHEW 4:6

Even Satan knew the Word. He told Jesus, "It is written," and quoted Psalm 91:11–12.

But Jesus knew the Word even better. With the authority of heaven He said, "It is written again, 'You shall not tempt the LORD your God'" (Matt. 4:7). Three separate times He said, "It is written" (Matt. 4:4, 7, 10). The third time Jesus finally said:

> Away with you, Satan! For it is written, "You shall worship the LORD your God, and Him only you shall serve."
>
> —MATTHEW 4:10

The enemy is still using the same tactics today. But the Lord Jesus defeated Satan with the power of the Word, and the same power is available to us today.

God's Word is a powerful weapon against the enemy's attacks because it reveals to us the conditions and promises of God's blood covenant. From the moment man sinned, God introduced the blood covenant as a means of covering, or atonement. In the next chapter we will see how it happened.

A COVENANT TO KEEP

1. Throughout history the blood covenant has been used in the natural as an expression of brotherhood or commitment between two individuals. It also served as a temporary means of atonement for sin under the old covenant.

   We can learn many spiritual lessons from a study of the blood. Although the blood covenant has even greater significance in the spirit realm, let's begin with a look at the first blood sacrifice recorded in Scripture. Read Genesis 3:21.

   Who made the decision to shed blood? Describe whose blood was shed and why:

   _____

   _____

2. Adam and Eve created chaos in their lives by disobeying God. They refused to acknowledge His complete sovereignty over their lives. They tried to play God instead of obeying God. Satan tempts us to disobey God's ways and do things our way. Read Exodus 20:1–17. These are the Ten Commandments given to Moses on Mount Sinai. This is a good point in this study for you to consider and examine your obedience to God. It is impossible to obey God without the power of the precious Holy Spirit and until we are fully surrendered to Jesus Christ as our Lord and Savior.

3. When Jesus shed His blood on the cross, He became the supreme sacrifice. The shed blood of Jesus gives you access to the throne of God anytime, anyplace, and in any circumstance. Describe what each of the following

passages says about the presence of God through the shed blood of Christ.

Hebrews 9:11–15

Hebrews 10:19–25

As the blood covers and cleanses you, Jesus makes you armed and dangerous through the mighty armor of God. You can withstand and defeat the wiles of the devil.

Pray the following prayer aloud, putting on God's armor and preparing for victory. Do this daily, putting on Jesus, putting on the blood, taking up the sword of the Spirit, and standing firm!

Lord Jesus, cleanse me and cover me with Your blood. I gird my loins with Your truth. I cover my heart with the breastplate of Your righteousness. I cover my feet, my walk in Your Spirit, with Your peace. I put on the helmet of Your salvation through Your shed blood. I take up the shield of faith, Your Word, with which I will defeat Satan through Your Word and blood. In the name of the Mighty Warrior, Jesus. Amen.

Chapter 3

The COVERING

WHEN ADAM AND Eve yielded to the snare of Satan, "the eyes of both of them were opened, and they knew that they were naked; and they sewed fig leaves together and made themselves coverings" (Gen. 3:7). Having lost their covering of God's glory, Adam and Eve tried in vain to cover themselves by sewing fig leaves together. The fact that they even tried to make clothes for themselves showed that they realized their need for a covering.

I am fully convinced that before the fall the first man and woman did not see their physical nakedness as shameful. They may have been without clothing as a means of covering, but I believe they were covered with the glory of God.

Because they were accustomed to being blanketed with God's glory, after they sinned they made themselves a covering (Gen. 3:7). When they first gained sight of self, they realized how empty and exposed they truly were and even "hid themselves from the presence of the LORD God among the trees of the garden" (Gen. 3:8).

The instant they yielded to temptation, they lost God-consciousness and gained self-consciousness. They lost sight of God and His glory. And at that point they tried through their own works to substitute the natural for the supernatural by being covered by fig leaves rather than God's glory, which they had known.

The Scriptures declare later that they heard the voice of God walking in the garden in the cool of the day saying, "Where are you?" (Gen. 3:8–9).

And Adam answered, "I heard Your voice in the garden, and I was afraid because I was naked; and I hid myself" (Gen. 3:10).

God wasn't inquiring as to their physical location in the garden.

He wanted to know, "Who told you that you were naked? Have you eaten from the tree of which I commanded you that you should not eat?" (Gen. 3:11).

Adam responded by blaming his wife and God when he said, "The woman whom You gave to be with me, she gave me of the tree, and I ate" (Gen. 3:12). When God asked the woman, she blamed the devil. "The serpent deceived me, and I ate" (Gen. 3:13).

Nothing has changed. Mankind still refuses to take the blame for anything. When there's a tragedy, God is still blamed. Insurance companies even avoid the financial responsibility for certain liabilities based upon "an act of God." The world blames God, and the church blames the devil. Yet sometimes it's neither God nor the devil who is responsible—it's you!

THE CHOICE

Adam lived in a perfect world. He had authority over God's creation and a personal relationship with God. Adam and Eve knew God intimately, for they had fellowshipped with Him regularly. As they walked and talked with God, they were given very simple instructions for living: "You can eat freely of every tree in the garden except the tree of the knowledge of good and evil. If you eat of that tree, you shall surely die." (See Genesis 2:16–17.)

Adam had everything he needed to exist. And he had authority over everything except the tree of the knowledge of good and evil. Although the serpent tempted Adam and Eve to do wrong, he could not force them to do anything against their will—it was their choice to sin. They were warned in advance of the consequences of disobedience: "If you eat of that tree, you shall surely die." The responsibility was theirs and theirs alone.

CURSES AND JUDGMENTS

Because of Adam and Eve's sin, God pronounced five separate curses and judgments:

1. God cursed the serpent. "So the LORD God said to the serpent: 'Because you have done this, you are cursed more than all cattle, and more than every beast of the field; on your belly you shall go, and you shall eat dust all the days of your life'" (Gen. 3:14).

2. God pronounced judgment on Eve. "I will greatly multiply your sorrow and your conception; in pain you shall bring forth children" (Gen. 3:16).

3. The Lord judged Adam and sentenced him to a life of toil. "Because you have heeded the voice of your wife, and have eaten from the tree of which I commanded you, saying, 'You shall not eat of it': Cursed is the ground for your sake; in toil you shall eat of it all the days of your life" (Gen. 3:17).

4. God cursed the ground. "Both thorns and thistles it shall bring forth for you" (Gen. 3:18).

5. Then the Lord sentenced Adam to eventual death. "In the sweat of your face you shall eat bread till you return to the ground, for out of it you were taken; for dust you are, and to dust you shall return" (Gen. 3:19).

In the midst of God's judgment, however, is a wonderful promise of redemption. The Lord said to the serpent:

I will put enmity between you and the woman, and between your seed and her Seed; He shall bruise your head, and you shall bruise His heel.

—GENESIS 3:15

The Lord declared that He was going to send the seed of the woman to bring deliverance. It was a promise fulfilled in the conquest of Christ on the cross over Satan. And that is a victory in which every believer shares.

THE FIRST SACRIFICE

Now when all these events took place, God did something marvelous. He initiated the first blood sacrifice.

We must remember that after Adam and Eve sinned, they ran from the presence of God. Previously clothed with His glory, they were now naked and ashamed. In desperation, they attempted to cover themselves with leaves.

That is when God selected some animals, perhaps lambs, and killed them.[1] He covered the man and woman with the skins of the slain animals (Gen. 3:21). I believe the animals had just been killed and the skins were still moist with blood when God used them to cover Adam and Eve.

> Unto Adam also and to his wife did the LORD God make coats of skins, and clothed them.
> —GENESIS 3:21, KJV

Please note: God's first sacrifice covered Adam and Eve's sin with animals' blood. As we will see, His final sacrifice covered you and me with the blood of His only begotten Son. When the Bible says, "It is the blood that makes atonement for the soul" (Lev. 17:11), the word *atonement* means "to cover." That is why I believe the shedding of blood had to be a part of the covering. When Adam and Eve sinned, they lost their close communion with God. But through the blood covenant, God was declaring that their sins were atoned for. The blood would one day bring back the fellowship and joy.

From the time of Adam to the time of Christ, Scripture is filled with numerous accounts of how God entered into a blood covenant. A few examples include the following:

Noah

Noah's first act after coming out of the ark when the floodwaters subsided was to make a blood covenant with the Lord. He did this by offering a sacrifice. He "built an altar to the LORD, and took of every clean animal and of every clean bird, and offered burnt offerings on the altar" (Gen. 8:20).

Abraham

Abraham was told by the Lord, "This is My covenant which you shall keep, between Me and you and your descendants after you: Every male child among you shall be circumcised" (Gen. 17:10).

Moses

Moses, after God delivered the commandments, gathered the people together and offered young bulls as a sacrifice. "And Moses took the blood, sprinkled it on the people, and said, 'This is the blood of the covenant which the LORD has made with you according to all these words'" (Exod. 24:8).

Abraham and Abimelech

Abraham and Abimelech sealed their relationship by covenant and the setting apart of seven ewe lambs (Gen. 21:22–32).

Jacob and Laban

The covenant between Jacob and Laban was sealed when "Jacob offered a sacrifice on the mountain, and called his brethren to eat bread. And they ate bread and stayed all night on the mountain" (Gen. 31:54).

Thousands of people have entered into a blood covenant like the one my father and Mr. Hanna made. In the Old Testament it was common for men to "cut a covenant" and make a pact through the shedding of blood.

Accounts of blood covenants are found not only in Scripture but also throughout history. The rite is still practiced by many tribes in Africa and societies in Asia, South America, and the Middle East.

The pact-until-death is entered into for a variety of reasons, from joining into a business partnership to protecting a weaker tribe from a stronger one. In many instances it has turned bitter enemies into lifelong friends.

STANLEY AND THE CHIEFTAIN

Henry Stanley was a journalist in the 1870s who traveled through the jungles of Africa in search of the famed missionary David Livingstone.

On numerous occasions Stanley observed the rite of blood brotherhood, or "strong friendship," to protect himself in his travels. Once he made a compact with Mirambo, the warrior chief of Western Unyamwezi.

Stanley first encountered the warrior chief when his expedition was defeated by Mirambo's forces during his initial search for Livingstone in 1871. He compared the chief's leadership in warfare to that of Napoleon and Frederick the Great.

During his second exploring expedition, Stanley hoped for a while to avoid Mirambo. But he became impressed by his powers and decided to meet him. He wanted to make strong friendship with him.

They met, and Stanley was quite taken with the warrior chief. The African hero and the heroic American agreed to make strong friendship with each other.

Stanley's "chief captain," Manwa Sera, was asked to seal the friendship of the two men by performing the ceremony of blood brotherhood between them.

Mirambo and Stanley sat facing each other on a straw carpet. Sera made an incision in each of their right legs, from which he extracted blood, and he interchanged it. He then exclaimed aloud:

If either of you break this brotherhood now established between you, may the lion devour him, the serpent poison him, bitterness be in his food, his friends desert him, his gun burst in his hands and wound him, and everything that is bad do wrong to him until death.[2]

At the end of the covenant, they gave a gift to each other in the usual ratification of the compact.

The same blood flowed in both Stanley's and Mirambo's veins. They were brothers and friends in a sacred covenant—life for life.[3]

Now, this was a pagan ritual and is in no way endorsed by Scripture. But let's look at the Bible and see the way God used blood in covenants with His people.

A COVENANT TO KEEP

1. From the time of Adam and Eve's disobedience in the garden, mankind has struggled to become free of the judgment of God. Even God's standard of the Law, given to Moses on Mount Sinai, was ineffectual to free man from the judgment of God. It was a standard that was impossible for man to keep because of his sinful state. (See Galatians 3:10–12.)

   Yet, in spite of the state of sin into which we are born, there is hope. Read Genesis 3:15 and describe God's promise in your own words.

   _____

   _____

2. Scripture is filled with accounts of how God entered into blood covenants with His people. Read each scriptural account in the chart below, and then describe what took place to initiate God's blood covenant with man.

Text	Person(s) Involved	Blood Sacrifice
Genesis 8:20		
Genesis 17:10		
Exodus 24:8		
Genesis 15:1–21		
Genesis 31:51–54		

3. Any sacrifice offered to God must be accompanied by a sincere, humble heart before God. Christ made one final blood sacrifice for us through His death on the cross. Today, our sacrifices involve worship and service. Nevertheless, there are several important principles that we need to understand about sacrificing to God. Some of these principles are listed below. Read each scripture and then, on each line, write the reference from the list below that matches each principle.

- 1 Samuel 15:22–23

- Psalm 50:7–15

- Amos 5:21–24

- Romans 12:1–3

- Psalm 4:5

- Psalm 51:14–17

- John 4:24

The Bible	The sacrifice God desires is...
	a broken, contrite heart.
	given with righteousness.
	not given out of rebellion, which is witchcraft.
	from true worship in spirit and truth.
	living sacrifices—changed lives.
	recognizing that God doesn't need our sacrifices.

The Bible	The sacrifice God desires is...
	our thanksgiving and praise.
	a sacrifice of righteousness to the Lord.

What is your heart attitude toward God? Confess any sin, any complacency, any empty tradition in your life. Pray to become a living sacrifice to the Lord. Pray Romans 12:1–2 for your life.

Dear Father, I will, by the mercies of God, present my body as a living sacrifice, holy, acceptable to God, which is my reasonable service. And I will not be conformed to this world, but I will seek to be transformed by the renewing of my mind, that I may prove what is that good and acceptable and perfect will of God. Amen.

Chapter 4

An ETERNAL COVENANT

THE BLOOD OF sacrifice can be seen throughout the Word of God from Genesis to Revelation and is a reminder and testimony of God's grace to man. From the beginning, blood has been involved in the covenant process.

As we saw in the previous chapter, the shedding of blood to provide a covering for sin was first seen in the Garden of Eden. After the fall of man, God could not look upon the first couple's sin, so Adam and Eve were clothed with the skins of animals sacrificed by God Himself. The blood-soaked skins provided a covering for their sin and presented a shadow of the eternal covenant that was to come when the blood of the Lamb of God would be shed as an eternal and everlasting sacrifice for sin.

Throughout the Old Testament we find many examples of the blood sacrifice and its importance in a person's relationship to God. The Old Covenant presented a shadow or type of what was to come. For example, each time the high priest entered into the holy of holies on the Day of Atonement, he offered blood sacrifices for his sins and the sins of the people. The blood of animals provided only a temporary covering or atonement for sin, for this act of atonement for sin was repeated each year as the high priest offered a blood sacrifice. Only when Jesus' blood was shed on Calvary was the work finished. His shed blood became the eternal covenant to redeem and reconcile man back to God.

As Jesus hung upon the cross, He said, "It is finished!" (John 19:30). Then He bowed His head and willingly gave His life as the supreme sacrifice. The work of redemption was completed once and for all, extending to eternity.

But did you know that Jesus shed His blood for us seven times, in fulfillment of the Mosaic covenant?

THE SEVEN SHEDDINGS OF JESUS' BLOOD

In Leviticus 16:11–14, God told Moses that the blood had to be sprinkled by Aaron, the high priest, over the mercy seat seven times. Jesus, our High Priest, fulfilled this commandment when He shed His blood seven times in Scripture. Let's take a closer look at each of these seven sprinklings, or sheddings, of His blood and what they mean for us as believers.

1. Gethsemane—He sweat drops of blood. The first shedding of blood is found in Luke 22:44, where Jesus is praying in Gethsemane on the night of His betrayal: "And being in agony, He prayed more earnestly. Then His sweat became like great drops of blood falling down to the ground."

Why did His sweat become as blood? So that we would be healed from within and our own souls would be healed. The Bible commands that we be made whole. Only by the blood can we be made whole. Jesus said, "Be made whole"—that's a command. You and I will be made whole when we understand the work of Calvary and the work of the blood of Jesus. This first shedding was for *our souls and the healing of our beings.*

2. House of Caiaphas—His face beaten and beard plucked out. Next let's look at Matthew 26:67: "Then they spat in His face and beat Him; and others struck Him with the palms of their hands." This aligns with Micah 5:1: "Now gather yourself in troops, O daughter of troops; He has laid siege against us; they will strike the judge of Israel with a rod on the cheek." Isaiah 52:14 says His face was marred more than any man's, and when you read this, you begin to see what happened. Isaiah 50:6 records, "I gave My back to those who struck Me, and My cheeks to those who plucked out the beard."

Here we see the second shedding of blood, when the Lord's face was so beaten by His enemies that it no longer looked human—and this is all before the cross, in the house of Caiaphas. Acts 20:28 says the blood of Christ purchased us. The blood of Jesus was the price for our salvation. The love of God was such that Jesus would stand there at the house of Caiaphas and shed His blood for us. This second shedding of His blood was for *our image, that we might "look" like Him.*

3. Before Pilate—His back scourged. The third shedding of blood is mentioned in Matthew 27:26: "Then he released Barabbas to them; and when he had scourged Jesus, he delivered Him to be crucified." Jesus' back was scourged (whipped), and the instrument of scourging in those days was an instrument of torture. Pieces of metal or sharp bones were tied onto the ends of the lashes, designed to tear the flesh open. "I gave My back to those who struck Me" (Isa. 50:6). That's why Isaiah said Jesus was marred in face and form more than any man.

The Lord offered His back of His own free will. He did not struggle. That is a picture of His love, isn't it? This third shedding of Jesus' blood was for *the healing of our bodies.*

4. Praetorium—A crown of thorns thrust on His head. In Matthew 27:27–29 we read:

> Then the soldiers of the governor took Jesus into the Praetorium and gathered the whole garrison around Him. And they stripped Him and put a scarlet robe on Him. When they had twisted a crown of thorns, they put it on His head, and a reed in His right hand. And they bowed the knee before Him and mocked Him, saying, "Hail, King of the Jews!"

Verse 28 says they put a scarlet robe on Jesus. I saw something so powerful one day that moved me deeply. In Genesis 3:17–19, when

Adam fell, God said, "Cursed is the ground for your sake; in toil you shall eat of it all the days of your life. Both thorns and thistles it shall bring forth for you, and you shall eat the herb of the field. In the sweat of your face you shall eat bread till you return to the ground."

Do you know what I found? There is a variety of thistle the same color as the robe they put on Jesus: scarlet. What did they put on the Lord's head? Thorns. What did He wear? A robe the color of thistles—the curse in Genesis. Jesus took upon Himself the curse that was placed on the planet.

The account in Matthew 27:29 says, "When they had twisted a crown of thorns, they put it on His head." But the word for *put* in the Greek means to make an assault, to attack—in this case, it meant to press the crown of thorns violently into His scalp until large amounts of blood flowed out. In Israel, the thorns have very long spikes on them, and they're as hard as nails.

Verse 30 tells us, "Then they spat on Him, and took the reed and struck Him on the head," and that is exactly what we saw in the Messianic prophecy of Isaiah 50. This fourth shedding of Jesus' blood was for *the healing of our minds.*

5. The cross—His hands nailed. In Matthew 27:35–37 we read, "Then they crucified Him, and divided His garments, casting lots, that it might be fulfilled which was spoken by the prophet: 'They divided My garments among them, and for My clothing they cast lots.' Sitting down, they kept watch over Him there. And they put up over His head the accusation written against Him: THIS IS JESUS THE KING OF THE JEWS." This fifth shedding of Jesus' blood was so that *our work might be accepted* (the work of our hands, our ministry, etc.).

6. The cross—His feet nailed. Psalm 22:16 says, "They pierced My hands and My feet," fulfilling the prophecy of the Old Testament. This sixth shedding of Jesus' blood was accomplished so that *our walk might be established—that we might walk with Him.*

7. The cross—His side pierced. The seventh and final shedding of blood was the piercing of His side. John 19:31–34 (KJV) reads:

> The Jews therefore, because it was the preparation, that the bodies should not remain upon the cross on the sabbath day, (for that sabbath day was an high day,) besought Pilate that their legs might be broken, and that they might be taken away. Then came the soldiers, and brake the legs of the first, and of the other which was crucified with him. But when they came to Jesus, and saw that he was dead already, they brake not his legs: But one of the soldiers with a spear pierced his side, and forthwith came there out blood and water.

The practice of breaking the legs was done so that those hanging on the crosses would die sooner, because in order to breathe they had to push up with their legs. When the soldiers came to the Lord and saw that He was already dead, they did not break His legs—fulfilling Psalm 34:20 and other scriptures, including Exodus 12:46. (Exodus 12 contains thirty-two prophecies that were fulfilled through the cross.)

In Psalm 34:20 we read, "He keepeth all his bones: not one of them is broken" (KJV). So when you read the preceding verse (v. 19), "Many are the afflictions of the righteous, but the LORD delivers him out of them all," it's talking about the Messiah. And then what follows? "He keepeth all his bones: not one of them is broken" (v. 20, KJV). This was fulfilled in John's eyewitness account of the crucifixion.

In John 19:35–37 John writes, "And he who has seen has testified, and his testimony is true; and he knows that he is telling the truth, so that you may believe. For these things were done that the Scripture should be fulfilled, 'Not one of His bones shall be broken.' And again another Scripture says, 'They shall look on Him whom they pierced'" (cf. Zech. 12:10).

John quoted Zechariah 12:10 because that scripture was fulfilled in his day, and he witnessed it. Prophetically speaking, why did they pierce Jesus' side? They pierced His side so that the church might be born. Isn't that precious, saints? So this seventh and final shedding of Jesus' blood was accomplished *that we might be born again.*

To summarize, the blood was shed in Gethsemane for our souls. The blood was shed from Jesus' face so that we could look like Him. The blood was shed from His back that we might be made whole. The blood was shed from His head that we might have His mind. The blood was shed from His hands that our work might be accepted. The blood was shed from His feet that our walk might be established. And finally, the blood was shed from His side that we might be born again.

To Him be all the praise, all the honor, and all the glory.

Because of the shed blood of Jesus, our sins are forgiven and we are guilty no more.

GUILTY NO MORE

Two years after I began in the ministry, I received a letter I will never forget from a lady who was extremely distraught. Although her letter did not provide many details, she wrote, "Please pray for me. I feel so horrible about the things I have done that I can't go on. I feel so guilty I just want to commit suicide."

I noticed there was a telephone number on the letter, so I said to my secretary, "I'd like to talk to this person. She sounds very desperate. See if you can get her on the phone."

My secretary reached the woman by phone and transferred the call to me. I identified myself to her, and I talked for a few minutes. Then I asked, "Why are you so troubled that you want to end your life?"

"I am ashamed to admit it," she said, "but I have committed adultery. I slept with five men, and the guilt I feel is so great that I just want to die."

"Are you born again?" I inquired.

"Yes," she said.

My immediate response was, "Have you repented? Have you asked the Lord to forgive you of your sin?"

"Yes, I have," she said.

"Do you believe God has forgiven you?"

There was silence on the other end of the line for a moment. Hesitating, she finally replied in a quiet voice, "I'm not sure."

"You need to know what the Bible says," I said. "If we truly repent of our sins, the blood of Christ totally cleanses us. Our past is erased. He not only forgives, but He has also chosen to forget our sins." I told her what God said in the Scriptures:

> I, even I, am He who blots out your transgressions for My own sake; and I will not remember your sins. Put Me in remembrance; let us contend together; state your case, that you may be acquitted.
>
> —ISAIAH 43:25–26

As I finished reading these verses, I added, "All you have to do is pray and ask God to forgive you. His Word promises that He will forgive and forget." Then I waited for a response from the woman at the other end of the line.

Finally she said, "Oh, but I feel so guilty. I can't even pray. I have committed too many sins."

I could hear her crying as she continued, "The guilt is unbearable. I can't even make myself go to church because I can't worship God. I would just rather die."

I interrupted her and asked, "How long ago did this happen?"

"Twenty-eight years ago," she sobbed.

I thought I had misunderstood, so I cautiously repeated, "When did you say this happened?"

"It happened twenty-eight years ago."

"Do you mean to tell me that you've been living with this guilt for twenty-eight years?" I asked.

"Yes," she blurted out, "and I can't bear it any longer. It's killing me!"

I called her by her name and asked, "Have you lived a clean life since then?" I waited for her to respond.

"Yes," she replied, "but even though I've never done anything like that since, I just can't live with the guilt."

I decided to get her attention. "Lady," I said, "listen to me. There's a bigger sin you must repent of. Do you realize that you have been grieving the Holy Spirit?" My words apparently caught her attention because her sobbing cries turned into a soft whimper as I continued. "It's the sin of not believing God's promises. He forgave you of the sin of adultery twenty-eight years ago when you prayed and asked Him to forgive you. But the devil has used that thing against you again and again, and now you feel so guilty you want to die because you don't think you have anything to live for. Quit insulting our wonderful Lord and the work of the cross. Quit insulting the cross by not accepting what He did for you."

"But," she said, interrupting me, "my sins are so great."

"The power of His blood to forgive and reconcile you back to God is greater!" I said boldly. "Every time you say, 'I don't believe Jesus will forgive me of my sin,' you are going against what the Word of God promises. You have to stop doubting and begin to believe what God's Word says. If you don't, you'll never live in victory. You are living a life of unbelief. God has given you His promise to bury all of your sins, and yet you refuse to believe it."

"What should I do?" she asked.

"Repent before the Lord, and ask Him to forgive you for not believing His promise. Jesus died for your sins. Why not give Him what He died for? Let's pray right now."

I will never forget praying with her on the telephone. I could sense the bondage lifting and the sunshine of God's love dawning upon her life. The woman was gloriously set free that day as she accepted what Jesus had done for her on the cross when He shed His precious blood for the remission of sin.

When we torment ourselves for past sin, it is like telling the devil, "Don't leave. I enjoy having you around." It is your guilt that keeps him lurking in the shadows of your life. But if you believe the Word of God and ask the Lord to cleanse you, forgive you, and deliver you from all sin, you will be set free from all that the enemy can bring against you.

A Covenant to Keep

1. Here are some truths from the Word about how to know and obey God's Word in your daily life. Read each text. Put a check mark next to each text you are obeying or applying. Circle each text that you need to obey or apply in your life.

   - "Keep this Book of the Law always on your lips; meditate on it day and night, so that you may be careful to do everything written in it. Then you will be prosperous and successful" (Josh. 1:8, NIV).

   - "But whose delight is in the law of the LORD, and who meditates on his law day and night" (Ps. 1:2, NIV).

   - "I have hidden your word in my heart that I might not sin against you" (Ps. 119:11, NIV).

   - "I will always obey your law, for ever and ever" (Ps. 119:44, NIV).

   - "I will walk about in freedom, for I have sought out your precepts" (Ps. 119:45, NIV).

   - "Your word is a lamp for my feet, a light on my path" (Ps. 119:105, NIV).

   - "If you love me, keep my commands" (John 14:15, NIV).

   - "All Scripture is God-breathed and is useful for teaching, rebuking, correcting and training in righteousness" (2 Tim. 3:16, NIV).

2. Ask the Holy Spirit to teach you the truths found in God's Word. Go back to the circles you drew earlier about Bible

truths you need to apply to your life. Spend some time making a prayer covenant with God to apply these truths.

Dear Father, I want to grow closer to You every day. Teach me from Your Word as I am faithful to read and study Your wonderful words of life. Thank You for making a way for me to be trained in righteousness. Amen.

Chapter 5

WHY a BLOOD COVENANT?

T HE FORGIVENESS WE received through Christ's suffering and death on the cross is certainly a marvelous thing. Nevertheless, the question of why God required the shedding of blood in the Old Covenant has been asked for generations. Why is the sacrifice of blood so important?

I have always been fascinated with the story of Cain and Abel, the first two sons of Adam and Eve. Scripture doesn't tell us how much time passed between Adam and Eve's departure from the Garden of Eden and the birth of their sons. However, from what the Bible does say about their birth, I think it's possible that Cain and Abel may have been twins. It says Eve conceived once and gave birth twice.

> Now Adam knew Eve his wife, and she conceived and bore Cain, and said, "I have acquired a man from the LORD." Then she bore again, this time his brother Abel.
>
> —GENESIS 4:1–2

Whether twins or siblings, it is very likely that after what Adam and Eve had experienced in the Garden of Eden, the children were taught the principle of presenting gifts to the Lord by their parents. As I have studied the scriptures that pertain to Cain and Abel, I have discovered how important the blood sacrifice is and how it relates to an individual's standing before God. This is illustrated through the offerings Cain and Abel presented to God.

> Abel was a keeper of sheep, but Cain was a tiller of the ground. And in process of time it came to pass, that Cain brought of the fruit of the ground an offering unto the LORD. And Abel, he also brought of the firstlings of his flock and of the fat thereof.
>
> —GENESIS 4:2–4, KJV

Scripture records that "the LORD respected Abel and his offering, but He did not respect Cain and his offering" (Gen. 4:4–5). What was the difference? Why did God accept one offering and reject the other? The answer is found in Hebrews 11:4:

> By faith Abel offered to God a more excellent sacrifice than Cain, through which he obtained witness that he was righteous, God testifying of his gifts; and through it he being dead still speaks.

It was "by faith" that Abel offered a blood sacrifice to the Lord. We know that "faith comes by hearing" (Rom. 10:17), so it's reasonable to assume the two sons knew the power of the blood because their parents shared their experience in the garden.

How did Abel know to offer a blood sacrifice? I believe Adam and Eve told their sons what God expected. I believe God gave a revelation of the blood covenant to the first man and woman when He sacrificed animals to atone for their sin and clothed them with skins that may have been wet with blood (Gen. 3:21). It was a sign of the redemption and deliverance that was to come. No doubt Eve wondered, "Which one of my sons will bruise the serpent's head?" (See Genesis 3:15.)

Both sons knew that God demanded a blood covenant. That is why God asked Cain, "Why are you angry? Why is your face downcast? If you do what is right, will you not be accepted?" (Gen. 4:6–7, NIV). Cain knew what was right, but he didn't do it. Instead he offered a gift of vegetation, and God refused it.

This was a crucial mistake. Cain knew from his parents'

experience what was acceptable as an offering, yet he decided to offer the fruit of his own hands, demonstrating his rejection of God's revealed covenant. Just as Adam's fig leaf covering was rejected and judged unacceptable by God after the fall of man, so for the same reason was Cain's offering: both were a product of their own works.

Abel, however, was obedient to the Lord, and his offering of a blood sacrifice was pleasing and acceptable to God. God had established the principle of the blood sacrifice in the Garden of Eden as a necessary requirement when approaching Him. And by faith Abel offered an animal sacrifice—the "firstfruits" of his flock. Though Cain's offering was rejected, God's acceptance of Abel's offering demonstrates the importance of a right standing before a covenant-making, covenant-keeping God. Abel's offering was from a heart of love and obedience.

Cain offered a gift, but it was not what God required. There is a great difference between presenting what the Lord demands and merely giving a present.

> Has the LORD as great delight in burnt offerings and sacrifices, as in obeying the voice of the LORD? Behold, to obey is better than sacrifice.
>
> —1 SAMUEL 15:22

AN UNTHINKABLE ACT

What was Cain's reaction to God's disapproval?

> So Cain was very angry, and his face was downcast. Then the LORD said to Cain, "Why are you angry? Why is your face downcast? If you do what is right, will you not be accepted? But if you do not do what is right, sin is crouching at your door; it desires to have you, but you must rule over it."
>
> —GENESIS 4:5–7, NIV

Here's what God was telling the disobedient son: "The choice is yours. You can make the decision to choose between right and wrong." It is a message that resounds throughout the Word of God. You and I have power over sin if we walk in faith and obedience to God.

But Cain ignored God's warning, and his next step was to commit an act that was unthinkable.

> Now Cain said to his brother Abel, "Let's go out to the field." While they were in the field, Cain attacked his brother Abel and killed him.
>
> —Genesis 4:8, NIV

The first murder in the Bible was committed with deliberate deceit. Cain called his unsuspecting brother out to a field and took his life. The killing was also the result of spiritual disobedience. He rebelled against presenting a blood covenant to the Lord.

What a contrast! The Word tells us that we "should love one another, not as Cain who was of the wicked one and murdered his brother. And why did he murder him? Because his works were evil and his brother's righteous" (1 John 3:11–12).

Immediately after the tragic event, the Lord asked Cain, "'Where is Abel your brother?' He said, 'I do not know. Am I my brother's keeper?'" (Gen. 4:9).

Cain's answer was more than an outright lie. It was a statement of indifference, even contempt.

Once again God spoke to Cain and asked, "What have you done? The voice of your brother's blood cries out to Me from the ground" (Gen. 4:10).

For years this portion of Scripture puzzled me. As I studied God's Word, however, I realized that when God said, "I hear your brother's blood crying out," it meant Abel's blood was crying out for vengeance and revenge. Abel's blood cried out for justice to be done. The blood of Jesus, speaking better things, cries out that justice has been done and our sins have been forgiven. Abel's blood cried out for vengeance; the blood of Jesus pleads for forgiveness and restoration.

As Christians we have come "to Jesus the Mediator of the new covenant, and to the blood of sprinkling that speaks better things than that of Abel" (Heb. 12:24).

Because of his sin, Cain would never know God's blessing. The Lord proclaimed this judgment:

> So now you are cursed from the earth, which has opened its mouth to receive your brother's blood from your hand. When you till the ground, it shall no longer yield its strength to you. A fugitive and a vagabond you shall be on the earth.
>
> —GENESIS 4:11–12

My friend, don't reject the message of the blood. It isn't worth the risk. Cain's punishment was for more than the murder of his brother. It was also because he disobeyed a revelation of God's blood covenant. Those who refuse God's covenant are in jeopardy of becoming hopeless wanderers, eternally lost.

The Bible makes it clear that if we reject Christ's blood, we have offended God's Holy Spirit.

> Anyone who has rejected Moses' law dies without mercy on the testimony of two or three witnesses. Of how much worse punishment, do you suppose, will he be thought worthy who has trampled the Son of God underfoot, counted the blood of the covenant by which he was sanctified a common thing, and insulted the Spirit of grace?
>
> —HEBREWS 10:28–29

The blood is not a topic to be shunned, ignored, or rebuffed. It is still our vital link to God.

THE PROMISE

One great blood covenant established in the Old Testament is called the Abrahamic covenant.

> The LORD appeared to Abram and said to him, "I am Almighty God; walk before Me and be blameless. And I will make My covenant between Me and you, and will multiply you exceedingly." Then Abram fell on his face, and God talked with him, saying: "As for Me, behold, My covenant is with you, and you shall be a father of many nations."
>
> —GENESIS 17:1–4

God reminded ninety-nine-year-old Abram of His covenant. The name Abram means "patriarch," and Abram had done everything he could in his own strength to help make God's covenant a reality.

When Abram's body was too old to produce, God reminded him of the covenant to "multiply him exceedingly."

> No longer shall your name be called Abram, but your name shall be Abraham; for I have made you a father of many nations. I will make you exceedingly fruitful; and I will make nations of you, and kings shall come from you. And I will establish My covenant between Me and you and your descendants after you in their generations, for an everlasting covenant, to be God to you and your descendants after you.
>
> —GENESIS 17:5–7

Abraham, the new name given to Abram by God, means "father of a multitude." God changed his name to one with a powerful meaning. It was intended to be a reminder of God's promise. Whenever Abraham heard himself or someone else say his name, he was reminded of God's promise to make him the father of a multitude and of many nations.

The Lord also promised to give Abraham and his descendants "the land of Canaan, as an everlasting possession" if they would keep the covenant (Gen. 17:8–9). Most important, this covenant would be marked by the shedding of blood.

> This is My covenant which you shall keep, between Me and you and your descendants after you: Every male child among you shall be circumcised; and you shall be circumcised in the flesh of your foreskins, and it shall be a sign of the covenant between Me and you.
>
> —GENESIS 17:10–11

What was the sign of the Abrahamic covenant? Circumcision. Every male child was to have this rite performed when he was eight days old. As a result he would not only enter into the covenant but also take part in God's promises to Abraham.

God honored the covenant He made with Abraham. At one hundred years of age, he and his wife, Sarah, who was ninety years old, conceived and produced a child of promise. They named him Isaac.

THE ULTIMATE TEST

After Isaac was born, God chose to test Abraham's faith in the covenant promise to make him the father of a great nation.

> Now it came to pass after these things that God tested Abraham, and said to him, "Abraham!" And he said, "Here I am." Then He said, "Take now your son, your only son Isaac, whom you love, and go to the land of Moriah, and offer him there as a burnt offering on one of the mountains of which I shall tell you."
>
> —GENESIS 22:1–2

The Lord was giving Abraham the ultimate test. When Satan tempts us, he wants to provoke us to evil. But when God tests us, He seeks to reinforce, strengthen, and fortify our commitment. Remember the difference: God tests us. Satan tempts us.

There was no question that Abraham's true affections were about to be exposed. Whom did he love more, Isaac or God? After all, the child had been given as a miracle. Would he love the gift more than the giver? The Bible says:

> Abraham rose early in the morning and saddled his donkey, and took two of his young men with him, and Isaac his son; and he split the wood for the burnt offering, and arose and went to the place of which God had told him. Then on the third day Abraham lifted his eyes and saw the place afar off. And Abraham said to his young men, "Stay here with the donkey; the lad and I will go yonder and worship, and we will come back to you."
>
> —GENESIS 22:3–5

When Abraham declared, "We will come back," he was demonstrating his total, unwavering faith and trust in God, for God had promised, "In Isaac your seed shall be called" (Gen. 21:12). Isaac's birth was a miracle. In the natural, there was no way for Abraham and Sarah to have a son. But God had been faithful to His covenant, and Abraham believed that "God was able to raise him up, even from the dead" (Heb. 11:19).

Even though Abraham had no idea of what was going to happen on that mountain, he had great faith in the covenant-making, covenant-keeping God.

> So Abraham took the wood of the burnt offering and laid it on Isaac his son; and he took the fire in his hand, and a knife, and the two of them went together. But Isaac spoke to Abraham his father and said, "My father!" And he said, "Here I am, my son." Then he said, "Look, the fire and the wood, but where is the lamb for a burnt offering?" And Abraham said, "My son, God will provide for Himself the lamb for a burnt offering." So the two of them went together.
>
> —GENESIS 22:6–8

When they reached the appointed place, Abraham built an altar and placed the wood in the proper place. As Isaac watched, he must have wondered where the sacrifice was. As a father, I can't imagine what must have been going through Abraham's mind as he "bound Isaac his son and laid him on the altar, upon the wood" (Gen. 22:9).

I can only imagine the emotions each of them felt when Abraham "stretched out his hand and took the knife to slay his son" (Gen. 22:10).

> But the Angel of the Lord called to him from heaven and said, "Abraham, Abraham!" So he said, "Here I am." And He said, "Do not lay your hand on the lad, or do anything to him; for now I know that you fear God, since you have not withheld your son, your only son, from Me."
>
> —Genesis 22:11–12

Abraham had passed God's test. He chose the giver over the gift. But the offering of blood still had to be presented.

> Then Abraham lifted his eyes and looked, and there behind him was a ram caught in a thicket by its horns. So Abraham went and took the ram, and offered it up for a burnt offering instead of his son.
>
> —Genesis 22:13

When we demonstrate our faith in God by our obedience, He not only promises to provide for us—He will provide!

Then the angel of the Lord called to Abraham a second time and said:

> Because you have done this thing, and have not withheld your son, your only son—blessing I will bless you, and multiplying I will multiply your descendants as the stars of the heaven and as the sand which is on the seashore; and your descendants shall possess the gate of their enemies.
>
> —Genesis 22:16–17

Because of Abraham's faith and obedience, God fulfilled His promise to make him the father of a great nation. And as Isaac and Abraham returned from the mountain, I can almost see Abraham with his arm around Isaac's shoulders, at times running his rugged hand through his son's hair. I'm sure a prayer of thanksgiving was on his lips and a song in his heart as he remembered his words of faith: "We will be back!"

THE EXODUS

While I was studying the blood covenant many years ago, the Lord showed me something very exciting. It was because of the Abrahamic covenant that God brought Israel out of Egypt.

> Now it happened in the process of time that the king of Egypt died. Then the children of Israel groaned because of the bondage, and they cried out; and their cry came up to God because of the bondage. So God heard their groaning, and God remembered His covenant with Abraham, with Isaac, and with Jacob.
>
> —EXODUS 2:23–24

Moses, before leading the great exodus, learned that God would punish those who did not keep the covenant. Evidently Moses failed to have one of his two sons circumcised. During a journey from his father-in-law's house back to Egypt, "it came to pass on the way, at the encampment, that the LORD met him and sought to kill him" (Exod. 4:24). The text is not clear whether God sought to destroy Moses or the son. But it is clear that Moses' wife, Zipporah, knew what caused God's wrath. She "took a sharp stone and cut off the foreskin of her son and cast it at Moses' feet....So He let him go" (Exod. 4:25–26).

It was a lesson the great leader would never forget. God will not honor a man who has broken His covenant.

As Moses led the children of Israel into the desert, the covenant was the binding force that held the great throng of people together. The Ten Commandments were much more than rules to live by. They became known as the Law of the covenant.

Try to imagine what it must have been like when Moses came down from Mount Sinai to the nearly two million waiting Israelites.

Moses told the people what God had declared, and they "answered with one voice and said, 'All the words which the LORD has said we will do'" (Exod. 24:3). It was an important step toward a new blood covenant between God and His people.

Early the next morning Moses built an altar at the foot of the mountain.

> Then he sent young men of the children of Israel, who offered burnt offerings and sacrificed peace offerings of oxen to the LORD. And Moses took half the blood and put it in basins, and half the blood he sprinkled on the altar. Then he took the Book of the Covenant and read in the hearing of the people. And they said, "All that the LORD has said we will do, and be obedient."
> —EXODUS 24:5–7

Then, standing before that great multitude, "Moses took the blood, sprinkled it on the people, and said, 'This is the blood of the covenant which the LORD has made with you according to all these words'" (Exod. 24:8).

Even the written covenant itself was consecrated. The writer of Hebrews says that "he took the blood of calves and goats, with water, scarlet wool, and hyssop, and sprinkled both the book itself and all the people" (Heb. 9:19).

When we honor our covenant with God, God will honor us. The remarkable story of Israel's wandering in the desert gives testimony to that fact.

> [He] fed you with manna....Your garments did not wear out on you, nor did your foot swell these forty years.
> —DEUTERONOMY 8:3–4

Why did God protect and provide for the children of Israel? Because they were a covenant people.

In the next chapter I want to show you how the blood of Jesus protects us from Satan today.

A COVENANT TO KEEP

1. Read 1 John 1:9. Christ offers us total forgiveness from all our sins—if we confess them to Him, He will cleanse us from all unrighteousness. Do not allow a "Cain" attitude to come between you and God. Don't let sin crouch at the door of your life, hindering your sacrifice, your offering, and your worship of God.

   Write a prayer confessing anything that may come between you and God. Thank Him for His forgiveness through the blood of Jesus.

   _____

   _____

2. Read the story of Israel's wandering in the desert. (See Deuteronomy 8:3–4.) God protected and provided for the children of Israel because they were a covenant people.

   Think of all the provisions God has prospered you with as you keep His covenant. He provides and prospers you under the blood of Jesus Christ. To help you remember how He prospers you, read Psalm 103. Using that psalm as a basis, list the provisions mentioned in the psalm that you are experiencing in your life right now.

   _____

   _____

3. One great blood covenant in the Old Testament is called the Abrahamic covenant—a circumcision of the flesh. (See Genesis 17.) Through Christ's sacrifice on the cross of Calvary, today we participate in circumcision of the heart.

Read Romans 2:25–29. How is the Holy Spirit leading you
to circumcise your heart?

_____

_____

Are you facing a test of your faith? Is something or someone
keeping you from surrendering all to receive the covenant of
promise? Pray the following prayer, adding the name of the person
or thing in the blank:

Lord, I surrender _____
*to You. I claim the fullness of Your promises for my life
through Your shed blood. Amen.*

Chapter 6

THERE'S PROTECTION in the BLOOD

IN 1975, ABOUT a year after I began preaching, I was invited to travel to the east coast of Florida to minister. One of the services was held at Indian Harbour Beach, Florida, in the home of my friend John Arnott, who is the founding pastor of Catch the Fire Church in Toronto (formerly Toronto Airport Christian Fellowship).

At the conclusion of my remarks I invited those who needed prayer to come forward. One woman brought her teenage daughter and asked me to pray for the girl. Just as I started to pray, I heard the clear voice of the Lord instruct me to do something I did not understand. He said, "Get the ring off her finger."

I was perplexed and thought, "What does the ring have to do with my praying for her?"

The Lord spoke again, even stronger. It was a command. "Get the ring off her finger."

Because nothing like this had ever happened to me before, I began questioning the voice. I wondered, "Is this really God?"

When I looked into the face of the young woman, I could see a soul that was in torment and deep bondage. When God spoke those words again, I reached out, took her by the hand, and asked, "What is this ring you are wearing?"

Then I pulled her hand closer to get a better look at the silver band around her finger. It had a little snake engraved on it—with the head showing and the body coiled around the band. When I looked at her, she had a puzzled expression on her face, as if to say, "What difference does it make? Go ahead and pray for me."

I was more bewildered than she was. All I knew was that the Lord had said, "Get the ring off."

I can still vividly recall this unusual encounter. I took my thumb and two fingers and tried to slide the ring from her finger. It was a loose-fitting ring, but somehow it would not budge. As I continued to pull, she began to scream. It wasn't a cry of pain but rather a loud, terrifying shriek. All the muscles in her body tightened.

Then an ugly, guttural voice spoke through her, chilling me to the marrow. "Leave her alone!" the voice shouted. "She's mine!"

The moment I heard those words, I knew God had given me the right instructions when He said, "Get the ring off her finger."

Holy anger surged within me because I knew I was in a battle against the power of Satan. I continued to pull on the ring. Two of the men in the room could see what was happening and held my shoulders as I waged this frightening but necessary battle for fifteen to twenty minutes.

Over her screams I finally cried, "I apply the blood of Jesus Christ!"

The moment I said those words, the ring came off her finger. Her rigid body relaxed, and her screeching turned into a sigh of relief. She was completely delivered and asked Christ to come into her heart. I believe the power of the blood of Jesus Christ cancels out any covenant made with the power of hell.

You may say, "Benny, do you believe the ring had anything to do with her condition?" Yes; because that ring symbolized her rebellion against God, I believe it was a symbol of a commitment to the forces of evil. The story of one of Israel's worst defeats helped me understand the danger of objects that we keep in disobedience to God's commands.

GET RID OF IT!

The story of Joshua and the Israelites' victory at Jericho is a familiar one to old and young alike. Even the lyrics of some songs refer to "the battle of Jericho" and the unconventional but God-inspired strategy that brought victory.

In the natural, I'm sure the prospect of victory seemed almost impossible as Joshua and the children of Israel surveyed the massive walls that surrounded the city of Jericho. But Joshua knew God's voice, and God had promised victory and laid out a very specific plan whereby this would come about.

God's instructions to Joshua are recorded in Joshua 6:2–5, which declares:

> And the LORD said to Joshua: "See! I have given Jericho into your hand, its king, and the mighty men of valor. You shall march around the city, all you men of war; you shall go all around the city once. This you shall do six days. And seven priests shall bear seven trumpets of rams' horns before the ark. But the seventh day you shall march around the city seven times, and the priests shall blow the trumpets. It shall come to pass, when they make a long blast with the ram's horn, and when you hear the sound of the trumpet, that all the people shall shout with a great shout; then the wall of the city will fall down flat. And the people shall go up every man straight before him."

In response to God's mandate, Joshua called the priests and organized the people as he had been instructed. The armed men went before the priests that blew the trumpets, followed by the priests carrying the ark of the covenant. Moments before this unusual procession began its first pilgrimage around Jericho, Joshua instructed the people, saying:

You shall not shout or make any noise with your voice, nor shall a word proceed out of your mouth, until the day I say to you, "Shout!" Then you shall shout.

—JOSHUA 6:10

Each day for six consecutive days the children of Israel marched quietly around the outer perimeter of Jericho. And as they returned to camp each evening, the walls of the city remained firmly on their foundation, as if defying anyone who might attempt to penetrate the walled fortress.

On the seventh day, the people were instructed to march around the city seven times. Just after the morning sun rose, the children of Israel took their first steps toward victory—one, two, three, four, five, six times around the massive stone walls of Jericho. And as they began the seventh trip around the city and the priests blew the trumpets, Joshua said to the people:

Shout, for the LORD has given you the city! Now the city shall be doomed by the LORD to destruction, it and all who are in it. Only Rahab the harlot shall live, she and all who are with her in the house, because she hid the messengers that we sent. And you, by all means abstain from the accursed things, lest you become accursed when you take of the accursed things, and make the camp of Israel a curse, and trouble it. But all the silver and gold, and vessels of bronze and iron, are consecrated to the LORD; they shall come into the treasury of the LORD."

—JOSHUA 6:16–19

As the trumpets blew and the people shouted, the walls crumbled and were leveled flat before the people. As they took the city, the promised victory was theirs.

Every man, woman, and child in Jericho, along with the animals, were destroyed. Only Rahab and her household were spared from the destruction that day, just as Joshua had instructed. As a result, the fame of Joshua and his incredible victory spread far and wide throughout the country.

Not long after the victory at Jericho, Joshua and the children of Israel faced another foe at the city of Ai. A few men were sent ahead to assess the strength of the enemy at Ai. Confident after the victory at Jericho, they told Joshua that compared to Jericho, Ai would be simple. In fact, they recommended that he send only two or three thousand men because the enemy numbered far less at Ai than at Jericho. Heeding their counsel, Joshua did as they recommended.

But when the two or three thousand men attempted to subdue and conquer the city of Ai, Scripture tells us that the men of Ai pursued them, killing some of the Israelites as they chased them away from the city gates and back toward Jericho.

As the battered, wounded warriors returned, fear and dismay swept through the camp. How could this noted, victorious band of conquering warriors have disintegrated into these battered, timid men? Surveying the situation, Joshua tore his clothes and fell on his face before the Lord and asked why this happened.

The Lord told him:

> Israel has sinned, and they have also transgressed My covenant which I commanded them. For they have even taken some of the accursed things, and have both stolen and deceived; and they have also put it among their own stuff.
>
> —JOSHUA 7:11

The offending soldier was Achan, of the tribe of Judah.

> And Achan answered Joshua and said, "Indeed I have sinned against the LORD God of Israel, and this is what I have done: When I saw among the spoils a beautiful Babylonian garment, two hundred shekels of silver, and a wedge of gold weighing fifty shekels, I coveted them and took them."
>
> —JOSHUA 7:20–21

It was only when Achan, his family, all his belongings, and the stolen items were destroyed that the curse on Israel was lifted and the covenant restored. And with the restoration of the covenant, victory came. Joshua and his men were able to subdue the enemy and capture the city of Ai (Josh. 7:25; 8:1–28).

God's message is clear. Be careful of what you allow into your home, for some things bring bondage. To Achan it was a Babylonian garment. To the girl it was a satanic ring worn in rebellion.

I believe God's protection is lifted when we walk in rebellion against His commands. The passage in Joshua 7:10–12 is very clear that you should not have an accursed thing in your home. God said to the children of Israel:

> Neither will I be with you anymore, unless you destroy the accursed from among you.
>
> —JOSHUA 7:12

If you travel overseas to some of the more primitive parts of the world, as I have, you see firsthand the demonstration of demonic powers in some cultures. However, demonic activity is not limited to the primitive parts of the world only.

As an American citizen, I want to point out that the United States is just as vulnerable to satanic influence and demonic activity as any other nation. I believe people can open themselves up to demonic powers when they indulge in activities like reading horoscopes or calling a psychic hotline. Individuals who visit palm readers and have their fortunes told, or those who watch demonic programs and movies, make themselves targets for Satan and his forces. Even individuals who play certain occultic board games put themselves at risk with demonic powers.

Over the course of my ministry I have encountered people who have experienced unexplainable demonic activity in their homes. In desperation they have sought counsel in helping to identify the problem. I can recall one family who owned an expensive piece of artwork of a false god. When they destroyed the statue, the demonic activity ceased, and peace returned to their home. For another individual it was a cultish book hidden away on a bookshelf, forgotten and out of sight. But as God revealed what the problem was and the book was removed, the evil presence in the home, which had seemed almost tangible, departed.

All these things open the door to demonic activity. Remember, Satan comes as an angel of light, but the Word of God says that he comes to kill, steal, and destroy. What may seem like a harmless activity can bring disaster and destruction upon a life. My advice to you is to read your Bible and listen to the voice of the Holy Spirit to avoid these pitfalls.

PROTECTION FROM PLAGUES

The authority of the blood covenant for protection is clearly seen in the example of the Egyptian plagues.

When the children of Israel were still slaves in Egypt, they cried to the Lord for deliverance. The Lord raised up Moses, who went before Pharaoh and told him, "The LORD God of the Hebrews has sent me to you, saying, 'Let My people go'" (Exod. 7:16).

But Pharaoh refused.

That same day God turned the Nile River into blood, but Pharaoh would not listen (Exod. 7:20).

Then the Lord sent plagues of frogs, gnats, flies, livestock disease, boils, hail, locusts, and darkness over the land. Chaos and unexplainable destruction were rampant throughout Egypt.

Finally God told Moses to warn Pharaoh to let the people go or one more plague would come upon Egypt.

> About midnight I will go out into the midst of Egypt; and all the firstborn in the land of Egypt shall die, from the firstborn of Pharaoh who sits on his throne, even to the firstborn of the female servant who is behind the handmill.
>
> —EXODUS 11:4–5

Again, Pharaoh refused to let the people go. God told Moses that the time had come for the deliverance of the children of Israel. It was such a momentous event that even their calendar should be changed. The Lord said, "This month shall be your beginning of months; it shall be the first month of the year to you" (Exod. 12:2).

God said, "This is your beginning," even though they were leaving a land that had almost been destroyed.

The Lord told Moses how the children of Israel would be spared from the death of the firstborn. Each family was to follow these seven instructions:

1. Choose a one-year-old male lamb or goat without blemish (Exod. 12:3–5).

2. Join together with small families that cannot use a whole lamb (Exod. 12:4).

3. Keep the lamb for four days before slaughter (Exod. 12:6).

4. Have the head of the household slay the lamb on the evening of the fourteenth day of the month (Exod. 12:6).

5. Sprinkle the blood of the lamb on the sides and the tops of the door frames of the house (Exod. 12:7).

6. Roast the lamb that evening, and eat it with bitter herbs and unleavened bread (Exod. 12:8).

7. Eat the meal in haste, with your cloaks tucked into your belts, sandals on your feet, and staves in your hands (Exod. 12:11).

God told them to prepare because He would pass over the land.

For I will pass through the land of Egypt on that night, and will strike all the firstborn in the land of Egypt, both man and beast; and against all the gods of Egypt I will execute judgment: I am the LORD.

—EXODUS 12:12

Then the Lord gave this promise:

Now the *blood* shall be a sign for you on the houses where you are. And when I see the *blood*, I will pass over you; and the plague shall not be on you to destroy you when I strike the land of Egypt.

—EXODUS 12:13, EMPHASIS ADDED

At midnight on the night of the Passover, the firstborn in every Egyptian household died. The wailing was heard across the land even before the sun rose (Exod. 12:29–30). But in the houses of the Israelites there was not one dead.

That first Passover was a shadow of what was to happen one day on a hill called Calvary. For at Calvary "Christ, our Passover, was sacrificed for us" (1 Cor. 5:7). There we were redeemed "with the precious blood of Christ, as of a lamb without blemish and without spot" (1 Pet. 1:19).

HELP FOR YOUR HOUSEHOLD

Why did the Lord tell the Israelites to find a lamb for the salvation of each household (Exod. 12:3)? I believe it is because the blessings of God's covenant can lead to salvation for an entire family.

Do you remember what God told Noah? He said, "Come thou and all thy house into the ark; for thee have I seen righteous before me in this generation" (Gen. 7:1, KJV). At the time this promise was given, Noah was the only pure and virtuous man the Lord could find. Yet God told him that his entire household would find protection because of his actions.

Also, in Genesis 19:29 we find that God delivered Lot out of Sodom because of His covenant with Abraham. The passage says,

"God remembered Abraham, and sent Lot out of the midst of the overthrow" (Gen. 19:29).

Centuries later, the Philippian jailer asked Paul and Silas, "Sirs, what must I do to be saved?" (Acts 16:30).

They told him, "Believe on the Lord Jesus Christ, and you will be saved, you and your household" (Acts 16:31).

I believe the Lord places special grace and protection on an entire house because of one person who comes into His kingdom. (See 1 Corinthians 7:14.) In the next chapter I will tell you how it happened in my own life.

A Covenant to Keep

1. It is very important that you examine your household to make certain that nothing accursed is under your roof. The following items and activities on this checklist could give the devil a foothold of attack and need to be removed from your house. These things open the door to demonic activity. My strong advice to you is to read your Bible and listen to the voice of the Holy Spirit to avoid these things.

   Check the items and activities on the list below that you have in your home or that you participate in regularly. Add any other things that you believe to be associated with demonic activity.

   ❑ Horoscopes

   ❑ Jewelry with astrological or occult symbols

   ❑ Books or magazines that contain materials from the occult or New Age movement

   ❑ Pictures that focus on the occult or New Age

   ❑ Phone calls to psychics

   ❑ Watching movies or videos with demonic, occult, or New Age themes, or horror films

   ❑ Playing New Age, heavy metal, or rock music

   ❑ Playing occult fantasy games

   ❑ Going to séances, palm readings, and other such events

   ❑ Becoming involved with cults or false religions

Other:

_____

_____

Other:

_____

_____

If you have checked anything on the list above, you need to take the following steps:

    a. Get rid of it.

    b. Repent, and ask the Lord to forgive and cleanse you through His blood.

    c. Ask the Holy Spirit to give you the power to resist future temptation.

    d. Read, study, and memorize God's Word.

    e. Rebuke the devil in Jesus' name, and apply the blood of Jesus over your home and family.

2. Why did the Lord tell the Israelites to find a lamb for each household (Exod. 12:3)? I believe it is because the blessings of God's covenant can lead to salvation for an entire family (1 Cor. 7:14). God has intervened to bring salvation to an entire family many times. The Bible gives us several examples. Read the following passages and describe what God said to righteous people about saving their households. Write down the name of the individual to whom God spoke.

Text	Individual	God's Words
Genesis 7:1		
Genesis 19:29		
Acts 16:30–31		
1 Corinthians 7:14		

Father, forgive me for allowing these demonic items to enter my home. I repent of any unconfessed sin in my life. Satan, I'm giving you an eviction notice: get out of my house in the name of Jesus! Right now I apply the blood of Jesus over my home, my family, and my life. Where there has been darkness, I pray that the light of Christ would come forth and dispel that darkness. In the mighty name of Jesus, amen.

Chapter 7

THERE'S
SALVATION
in the BLOOD

I DID NOT REALIZE it as a child, but from the early days of my childhood in Israel our family was involved in a number of activities that were more pleasing to Satan than to God. A fortune teller regularly visited our house to read my mother's palm. In Toronto a woman named Victoria would often read her coffee cup.

Most Israelis drink strong coffee in little cups. After the coffee is gone, little grounds remain. By tipping the cup over, the grounds form a pattern. The woman, supposedly an expert in such matters, came by to read the pattern and predict what was going to happen.

When I tried to warn my family that these activities were ungodly, they only laughed at me. In their minds it was a harmless activity that had been a part of our home and our traditions for years.

I remember one night in particular, more than two years after I gave my life to Christ, when I came home from church. An unusual, oppressive feeling was in the house. When I got into bed, I began to hear noises downstairs—the refrigerator door being slammed shut, dishes breaking, and the sound of horrible laughter.

Immediately I prayed, "Lord, cover me with Your blood. Please protect me."

I heard what sounded like footsteps running through the back door and out of the house. I held my breath and waited for a moment. Then I cautiously went downstairs. I was relieved to discover no one was there. Some individuals may not understand this. They may never have been exposed to anything of this nature. I assure you, the demonic realm and demon powers are very real. The Scriptures have a great deal to say about how demons operate. Matthew 12:43–45 provides some insight into this area and indicates that demons

- get tired and seek rest;

- search for a dwelling place;

- have memories;

- have intelligence; and

- work together.

Many other stories in the Gospels and the Book of Acts show us demons are real (Luke 4:36; 8:26–37; Acts 19:13–16).

As you study Luke 8:26–37, you find a man who was known to have demons a long time. Tormented and uncontrollable, he had been bound with chains and fetters, but he had fled to the wilderness after breaking the chains. When Jesus encountered him, the demon-possessed man was naked and living among the tombs like an animal. The Bible tells us:

> When he saw Jesus, he cried out, fell down before Him, and with a loud voice said, "What have I to do with You, Jesus, Son of the Most High God? I beg You, do not torment me!"… Jesus asked him, saying, "What is your name?" And he said, "Legion," because many demons had entered him.
>
> —LUKE 8:28, 30

Jesus commanded the demons to leave the man, casting them into a herd of pigs nearby. The Bible tells us that when the demons entered into the pigs, the swine ran down a steep embankment, violently hurling themselves into a lake, and were drowned. Eyewitnesses to the miraculous deliverance were frightened and fled. Later, they came to Jesus "and found the man from whom the demons had departed, sitting at the feet of Jesus, clothed and in his right mind" (Luke 8:35).

Jesus had power and authority over demons, and through the Lord Jesus Christ and His mighty name that same power is available to every believer. Luke 10:19 says:

> Behold, I give you the authority to trample on serpents and scorpions, and over all the power of the enemy, and nothing shall by any means hurt you.

Furthermore, John wrote:

> He who is in you is greater than he who is in the world.
> —1 JOHN 4:4

The experience that night in our home taught me a valuable lesson. I discovered that as soon as I prayed, "Lord, cover me with Your blood," the footsteps and eerie sounds downstairs ceased. The promised power and authority over the power of the enemy referred to in Scripture was a reality. The promised authority was mine. All I needed to do was learn how to appropriate it.

Then one day the Lord said to me, "Use your authority as a believer." He was reminding me that as a Christian I had authority over Satan. As it says in Revelation 12:10–11:

> The accuser of our brethren, who accused them before our God day and night, has been cast down. And they overcame him by the blood of the Lamb and by the word of their testimony.

That evening as I began to comprehend the magnitude of the authority available to me as a believer, I boldly commanded Satan to take his hands off my family. Day after day I prayed for every member of my family.

I learned later that on that same night, the Lord appeared to my mother in such a powerful dream that from that moment on she never invited another fortune teller to our home. I didn't know it at the time, but God was already working in the hearts of my family members as I took my authority in prayer as a believer.

Not long afterward, I was scheduled to preach in a little church on the west side of Toronto. The Lord was just beginning to use me, and I took advantage of every opportunity to preach that was afforded to me. Yet, as the only Christian in my family, I never mentioned my preaching at home. I didn't dare.

As I got ready for the service, I was filled with excitement. The call of God burned deep within me, and I couldn't wait to get to the church and share what God had put in my heart.

The church wasn't very big, but that didn't matter to me. Seated on the platform, I sang along during the song service, enjoying the songs of worship. At one point I looked up, and I couldn't believe my eyes. Could it be possible? Did I see my mother and father seated at the back of the auditorium?

I turned my head. Next to me sat Jim Poynter, my dear friend and spiritual father. "It's not a dream," I thought. "Jim is sitting here next to me. This must be happening."

I looked down at my Bible for a moment and then quickly scanned the audience once more. It was them! I didn't know how or why, but my parents were really there!

I leaned over in Jim's direction and said, "Pray, Jim...please pray!" as I gestured in the direction of my parents seated at the back of the sanctuary. As he looked in the direction I had indicated, his eyes revealed his surprise at their presence as well.

A HEDGE OF PROTECTION

When you ask God to cover your family with the blood of His Son, I believe the Lord then builds a hedge of protection in the spiritual realm around your home. That is what He did for Job.

The Bible states that Job was a righteous man, "blameless and upright, and one who feared God and shunned evil" (Job 1:1). God made him a prosperous man, with thousands of sheep, camels, oxen, and other possessions. He was called "the greatest of all the people of the East" (Job 1:3).

But Job was concerned about the lifestyles of his children. His seven sons would take turns holding feasts in their homes, and they would invite their three sisters to eat and drink with them.

Job was so troubled about their spiritual condition that when the days of feasting were over:

> Job would send and sanctify them, and he would rise early in the morning and offer burnt offerings according to the number of them all. For Job said, "It may be that my sons have sinned and cursed God in their hearts." Thus Job did regularly.
>
> —JOB 1:5

One day some angels presented themselves to the Lord, and Satan was among them.

> And the LORD said to Satan, "From where do you come?" So Satan answered the LORD and said, "From going to and fro on the earth, and from walking back and forth on it." Then the LORD said to Satan, "Have you considered My servant Job, that there is none like him on the earth, a blameless and upright man, one who fears God and shuns evil?" So Satan answered the LORD and said, "Does Job fear God for nothing? Have You not made a hedge around him, around his household, and around all that he has on every side?"
>
> —JOB 1:7–10

Job did exactly what God had instructed. He applied the blood, and he did it "regularly" (Job 1:5). Do you realize that through prayer, the blood can be applied for your family? God will honor your faith.

Job covered his family with the blood by offering a sacrifice. In the New Testament the sacrifice has been made once and for all through Jesus Christ. So how do we take advantage of what He has done for us?

First, we must believe in the sacrifice He already made, the blood He already shed. When we believe, then we can speak it to God in prayer. The apostle Paul said, "We also believe and therefore speak" (2 Cor. 4:13). But there is no magic formula or phrase that activates the power of the blood. It is only by faith in Jesus Christ.

APPLYING THE BLOOD THROUGH PRAYER

Do you want to live in victory and be free from bondage? The key is to obey God's Word. Prior to the first Passover, the Lord said, "The blood shall be to you for a token upon the houses where ye are" (Exod. 12:13, KJV). The word *token* means evidence or a sign in the Hebrew. God protected the households that had the sign. As you apply the blood in prayer, He sees the sign and will protect you.

People have asked, "Why should we ask God to cover us with the blood every day? Isn't this vain repetition? Aren't we being superstitious? Aren't we acting out of bondage?"

I don't pray every day because I must pray. I commune with the Lord because I love Him and want to talk with Him on a daily basis. I also ask the Holy Spirit to fill me anew every day. Asking the Lord to cover me with the blood continually is not because of bondage but because of relationship and fellowship.

As Kathryn Kuhlman once said, "We don't live on yesterday's glories, nor on tomorrow's hopes, but on today's experiences."

You may ask, "What does being covered with the blood mean?" It means we are appropriating all the benefits of the cross of Jesus Christ: protection, access, forgiveness, security in God's grace, redemption, reconciliation, cleansing, sanctification, dwelling in God's presence, and victory.

I don't become born again daily. But every morning I surrender again my body and mind to Him. Asking Him to cover me with His blood is not a ritual or a religious "rabbit's foot" but the result of a relationship He has with me through the blood covenant.

The blood does not cover you automatically. God does not reach down from the sky and place the mark on the doorposts of your dwelling place. You have to ask for His protection. Remember that God supplies, but we apply through our believing prayer. The children of Israel took the blood "and put it on the two doorposts and on the lintel of the houses" (Exod. 12:7).

FOREVER!

The Word of God is indispensable to our knowledge and to our faith in God. We need to gain the greatest knowledge of the Word possible. The Word and the blood work together. The Word says, and the blood does.

The evil one may fight you at every turn, but when you apply the blood, God's power comes alive.

As a minister, I have preached on countless topics, but each time I preach on the blood, three things happen:

1. Satan makes every attempt to distract me from my preparation on the topic.

2. The devil tries his best to disturb the meeting itself.

3. An unusual presence of the Lord accompanies the message, and a large number of people find Christ as Savior.

Just as some ministers have never preached a sermon on the blood, some Christians have rarely uttered the word *blood* since their conversions. The subject seems to be totally erased from their minds. But God specifically instructed the Israelites to observe the Passover "as an ordinance for you and your sons forever" (Exod. 12:24). Forever means *forever*!

The Lord has never changed His mind about His blood covenant with His people. It was not limited to the forty years that the children of Israel journeyed to the Promised Land. The command was in effect even after they reached their destination.

> It will come to pass when you come to the land which the LORD will give you, just as He promised, that you shall keep this service.
>
> —EXODUS 12:25

We have even more to celebrate. God replaced the blood of sheep and goats with the perfect sacrifice, the blood of His precious Son Jesus Christ. By the same token we are to celebrate His covenant forever.

You may ask, "Benny, how often should we ask God to cover us with the blood?"

I personally do it every time I pray.

There is not a day I do not in prayer say, "Lord, cover Suzanne, Jessica, Natasha, Joshua, and Eleasha with Your blood." I do the same thing with each one of them separately. If I'm traveling, I call them on the phone and pray with them and continually pray that their hearts and minds will be filled with the Lord.

Several years ago I overheard my Tasha praying. She didn't know I was listening. I put my head to the door, which was slightly ajar. I was moved as I heard her saying, "Now, Lord, You shed Your blood for us, and I ask You to cover all of us." And she prayed for us one by one. There was another time when she said, "Now, Satan, you hear me real good: You can't touch me. The blood is covering me."

That's why it's so wonderful when parents ask the Lord to protect their children with the blood. Their children not only copy them but actually will ask questions about it. Then the parents have the opportunity to tell their children what the Lord has done.

My daughter Jessica is now a beautiful, grown young lady. Yet I can still remember when she reached the age to ask, "Daddy, why do you do that?"

I was able to tell her about the Passover story and how the blood of Jesus had been shed for us. If the blood of an animal could protect a family then, how much more can the blood of Christ protect us now?

"DON'T SAY THAT!"

In 1992 I preached a crusade in the city of Manila in the Philippines. One night they brought up to the platform a young man who seemed deeply troubled.

Suddenly, as this young man came close to me, I could see that he was demon-possessed. His eyes were glazed, and his whole figure began to change right in front of me. The closer he came, the worse he got.

I started praying, and he fell forward. Then this young man got up and started coming at me. Some of my assistants were trying to hold him back, but he threw them out of the way. I rebuked him, but he kept coming. Finally two very strong men were able to keep him in one place, but he was still fighting hard.

I said, "Lord, cover me and everyone around me with the blood of Jesus." Then I said to him, "The blood of Jesus is against you."

The second I said that, he screamed, "Don't say that!"

So I said it again, "The blood of Jesus is against you."

In a horrible voice he screamed emphatically, "Don't say that!"

Every time I spoke of the blood of Jesus, he would have a violent reaction. Thank God, he was finally set free.

Demons recognize the power of the blood of Jesus. If demons know it, then how much more should we know it?

I believe that when we ask God to cover us with the blood of Jesus, He honors that because it represents the name of Jesus and the authority connected with that name.

The power is in Jesus Christ, and we have access through prayer.

PRAYER POWER

A young man who attended my church in Orlando once asked, "What's the secret? What can I do to pray with more power?"

I told him, "Jesus gave us the answer when He said, 'If you abide in Me, and My words abide in you, you will ask what you desire, and it shall be done for you'" (John 15:7).

I said to him, "Notice what the Lord said—'If you abide in Me.' It's our choice, then, to abide. The verse goes on to say, 'And My words abide in you, you will ask...' You will ask because you have decided to abide in Him and you have chosen His Word to abide in you. That's the secret of power in prayer."

All things are possible through prayer.

One of the greatest teachers on prayer was R. A. Torrey. Torrey, who lived from 1856 to 1928, was the pastor of the famous Moody Church in Chicago for twelve years. In my early years as a Christian, I was deeply influenced by his writings and the writings of two other great preachers—D. L. Moody and Charles Finney.

Torrey, in his book *How to Obtain Fullness of Power*, says:

> Prayer can do anything God can do; for the arm of God responds to the touch of prayer. All the infinite resources of God are at the command of prayer.[1]

He also says:

> There is only one limit to what prayer can do; that is what God can do. But all things are possible to God; therefore prayer is omnipotent.[2]

E. M. Bounds, a turn-of-the-century preacher who is well known for his books on prayer, said:

> Only God can move mountains, but faith and prayer move God.[3]

I believe prayer is faith passing into action. When we pray, all that God is and has becomes ours. All you need to do is ask. As the Bible says, "Ye have not, because ye ask not" (Jas. 4:2, KJV). I've heard it said, "The strongest one in Christ's kingdom is he who is the best knocker."

> So I say to you, ask, and it will be given to you; seek, and you will find; knock, and it will be opened to you. For everyone who asks receives, and he who seeks finds, and to him who knocks it will be opened.
>
> —LUKE 11:9–10

As we knock at the door in prayer, God hears and answers our prayers because the blood of Jesus has cleansed us from our sins and provided access to the throne of God. So, start knocking and expect the answer.

A Covenant to Keep

We have to ask for God's protection. Remember, God supplies, but we apply through our believing prayer. The children of Israel took the blood "and put it on the two doorposts and on the lintel of the houses" (Exod. 12:7).

1. Where do you need to apply the blood over your relationships and your possessions? Using the list below of benefits available through the blood of Jesus, think of a person you know who needs each benefit. List that person's name by the benefit, and then pray to apply the blood to that person's life.

Person's Name	I apply the blood that he/she may...
	know God's protection.
	know God's forgiveness.
	know reconciliation.
	know God's cleansing power.
	overcome insecurity, doubts, or fears.
	experience sanctification.
	know God's presence.
	overcome temptation.

Take the time now to pray for each person that you named. Expect each person to experience Christ's grace and victory in their lives because of the covering of His blood.

2. Here are some important verses from the Word that you can use to speak to the enemy to claim victory over his attacks. Summarize what each verse says to the enemy.

The Word	To the enemy I declare...
Psalm 52:5	
Romans 16:20	
Ephesians 6:10–13	
James 4:7–10	
1 John 3:8; 4:4	

3. Now is the time for you to put your faith into action. Pray. Ask the Lord to cover you, protect you, and give you victory through the blood. Complete the following sentences, inserting the names and needs of your family.

- I ask the Lord through His blood to cleanse

_____

- I ask the Lord through His blood to forgive

_____

- I ask the Lord by His blood to cover

_____

- I ask the Lord by His blood to protect

_____

- I ask for victory through Jesus' blood for

_____

How is your prayer power? Do you pray in power through the blood of Christ, or do you simply utter vain repetitions to God?

E. M. Bounds said, "Only God can move mountains, but faith and prayer move God." I believe that prayer is faith passing into action. Only as we pray and trust, by faith, in the blood of Jesus will the mountains that we face in our lives move.

No matter what obstacles you may be facing today, as you pray in faith those mountains will be removed. Take a moment to write down the problems you are facing today. Then, in prayer, command them to be removed in Jesus' name as you apply the blood to each situation.

_____

_____

Chapter 8

THERE'S CLEANSING in the BLOOD

WHEN GOD GAVE the ordinances in the Old Testament, He spoke to Moses regarding "the law of the leper for the day of his cleansing" (Lev. 14:2). The Levitical instructions for the cleansing of leprosy provide a wealth of insight into the power of Christ's blood.

In Scripture, leprosy refers to a variety of skin diseases. It is also a symbol of sin. So the cleansing of the leper foreshadowed God's future plan to cleanse all of mankind from sin.

First, the leper to be cleansed was "brought to the priest" (Lev. 14:2).[1]

The priest was instructed to go outside the city and "take for him who is to be cleansed two living and clean birds, cedar wood, scarlet, and hyssop" (Lev. 14:4).

Each of these elements reminds me of the work of Christ for the remission of sin. The priests going outside the camp point to Jesus being crucified outside the walls of Jerusalem. I believe the two birds foreshadow the Lord's death and resurrection. Cedar wood points to the cross, and scarlet to His suffering.

Finally, hyssop symbolizes faith. David said:

> Purge me with hyssop, and I shall be clean; wash me, and I shall be whiter than snow.
>
> —PSALM 51:7

80

The hyssop that was used in purification ceremonies is generally considered to be a fragrant plant from the marjoram family.[2] It symbolizes faith to me because it was used in the application of the blood (Exod. 12:22).

What happened next was amazing in light of what Christ would do at Calvary.

> Then the priest shall order that one of the birds be killed over fresh water in a clay pot. He is then to take the live bird and dip it, together with the cedar wood, the scarlet yarn and the hyssop, into the blood of the bird that was killed over the fresh water.
>
> —LEVITICUS 14:5–6, NIV

When the first bird was killed, the blood was caught in an earthen vessel with water in it. This speaks of Christ's shedding His blood in an earthen vessel—His human body.

Then the priest took the living bird along with the cedar wood (Christ's cross), the scarlet (His suffering), and the hyssop (faith) and dipped them in the shed blood of the bird that was slain.

The slain bird's blood was mixed with the water in the earthen vessel, symbolizing cleansing by the Word (Eph. 5:26).

Here was the final instruction:

> Seven times he shall sprinkle the one to be cleansed of the defiling disease, and then pronounce them clean. After that, he is to release the live bird in the open fields.
>
> —LEVITICUS 14:7, NIV

This speaks of our sins being cleansed by the blood. Then we see the resurrection in the living bird that was released.

This cleansing ceremony is just one example of the way the Old Covenant foreshadows the New Covenant. Paul told the Colossians that no one should judge them according to the Old Covenant traditions about eating, drinking, and festivals because the Law was a "shadow of things to come, but the substance is of Christ" (Col. 2:16–17). Hebrews also says that the Law had a "shadow of the good things to come" but not "the very image" (Heb. 10:1).

The leper was then allowed to come into the camp (Lev. 14:8). In the same way, when you have been cleansed and purified by Christ's blood, you are ready to enter God's kingdom.

I believe the priests sprinkled the leper with blood seven times for a prophetic reason, because the blood of Christ was shed seven different times during the hours surrounding His crucifixion, as we saw in chapter 4. Here's a brief recap:

1. *His sweat.* "And being in agony, He prayed more earnestly. Then His sweat became like great drops of blood falling down to the ground" (Luke 22:44).

2. *His face.* "I gave...My cheeks to those who plucked out the beard" (Isa. 50:6).

3. *His head.* "When they had twisted a crown of thorns, they put it on His head, and a reed in His right hand. And they bowed the knee before Him and mocked Him, saying, 'Hail, King of the Jews!' Then they spat on Him, and took the reed and struck Him on the head" (Matt. 27:29–30).

4. *His back.* "Then he [Pilate] released Barabbas to them; and when he had scourged Jesus, he delivered Him to be crucified" (Matt. 27:26).

5. *His hands.* "For dogs have surrounded Me; the congregation of the wicked has enclosed Me. They pierced My hands" (Ps. 22:16).

6. *His feet.* "They pierced...My feet" (Ps. 22:16).

7. *His side.* "But one of the soldiers pierced His side with a spear, and immediately blood and water came out" (John 19:34).

THE CLEANSING CONTINUES

What happened after the leper was sprinkled seven times with blood? He was pronounced clean and could enter the camp, even as once we are cleansed by His blood we become sons and daughters of the living God and members of His family.

Because of the blood of Jesus, the floodgates of God's anointing can be released through His Holy Spirit in our lives. That's what I learned when the Holy Spirit visited me and transformed my life forever.

A COVENANT TO KEEP

1. The cleansing of the leper in the Old Testament (Lev. 14:2) foreshadowed God's future plan to cleanse all of mankind from sin by the blood of Christ. Read each Scripture portion listed below. Journal the similarities and symbolism of each step in the process of cleansing.

Scripture	OT Action	NT Similarity
Leviticus 14:2		
Leviticus 14:4		
Leviticus 14:5–6		
Leviticus 14:7		
Leviticus 14:8		

2. Write a personal prayer asking for cleansing from your sins through the blood of Christ. Ask God to reveal to you hidden areas of sin that you have been unwilling to confront or are unaware of their existence.

_____

_____

THERE'S POWER
IN THE BLOOD

PART II WILL focus on operating in the power of the blood. Once we are transformed by its cleansing power, we walk in newness of life, divine anointing, and freedom to minister. There is also strength for the weak and rest for the weary in the blood of Christ. We conclude by showing the significance of Holy Communion and how partaking of Communion is more than just a symbolic ritual; it is a time to get to know Him more intimately.

Chapter 9

TRANSFORMED
by the POWER

A S I SHARED in my book *Good Morning, Holy Spirit*, it was three days before Christmas 1973 when the Holy Spirit entered my bedroom in Toronto as I knelt beside my bed in prayer. I was only twenty-one years old and had just returned from a Kathryn Kuhlman meeting in Pittsburgh.

The seven-hour bus ride back to Toronto had been exhausting, but the excitement of what I experienced at the Kathryn Kuhlman service made it impossible for me to sleep. Kneeling in the darkness of my bedroom, I whispered, "Holy Spirit, Kathryn Kuhlman says You are her friend. I don't think I know You." Then, with my hands raised, I asked, "Can I meet You? Can I really meet You?"

I waited, but nothing happened. For ten long minutes I knelt beside my bed and quietly waited. Just as I was about to give up, something incredible happened. The presence of the Holy Spirit rushed into my room with such power that I began to tremble. A wonderful warmth enveloped my body, and I felt as though I had been wrapped in a thick blanket of love. The dimension of love I experienced was so glorious and brought such ecstasy to my soul that for a moment I thought I must be in heaven.

The presence of the Holy Spirit there in my bedroom was so rich. As I lingered in His presence, my thirsty soul drank from a well overflowing with living water. Minutes slipped into hours, and I lost all awareness of time. His presence was all that mattered.

I can still remember that night as if it were yesterday. My life was transformed as the Holy Spirit came into my room with such an undeniable presence that December night fifty years ago. From that moment the Holy Spirit was no longer a detached, distant "third Person" of the Trinity. He was real, more real to me than the things around me. And as I spent time in His presence in the days and weeks that followed, He became my closest Friend, my Comforter, and my Guide.

Later as I studied the Bible day after day, God began to reveal to me through His Word that it was the shed blood of Jesus Christ that made it possible for the Holy Spirit to descend.

Scripture records the words of Jesus to His disciples when He said:

> Nevertheless I tell you the truth. It is to your advantage that I go away; for if I do not go away, the Helper will not come to you; but if I depart, I will send Him to you.
>
> —JOHN 16:7

On the day of Pentecost, Peter spoke of the Lord's death and resurrection. He continued:

> Therefore being exalted to the right hand of God, and having received from the Father the promise of the Holy Spirit, He poured out this which you now see and hear.
>
> —ACTS 2:33

Remember that man's redemption from sin was made possible through Christ's death and resurrection. The Word of God tells us that following His resurrection, Jesus ascended to His Father and there presented the blood, which was the evidence of redemption.

> But Christ came as High Priest of the good things to come, with the greater and more perfect tabernacle not made with hands, that is, not of this creation. Not with the blood of goats and calves, but with His own blood He entered the Most Holy Place once for all, having obtained eternal redemption.
>
> —HEBREWS 9:11–12

When the Father accepted the blood, I believe Christ Jesus received from the Father the gift of the Holy Spirit to pour out upon those who believed in Him.[1] And now the Holy Spirit is on earth to enable us to live the Christian life, for God speaking through Ezekiel said:

> I will give you a new heart and put a new spirit within you; I will take the heart of stone out of your flesh and give you a heart of flesh. I will put My Spirit within you and cause you to walk in My statutes, and you will keep My judgments and do them.
>
> —EZEKIEL 36:26–27

The Holy Spirit not only enables us to live the Christian life, but He will also make God's presence very real to us.

> "And I will not hide My face from them anymore; for I shall have poured out My Spirit on the house of Israel," says the LORD God.
>
> —EZEKIEL 39:29

My first encounter with the Holy Spirit was glorious. Even though I had never experienced anything like that before, I should not have been surprised when my life was utterly and completely transformed by His power. That is exactly what happens when you and I have a face-to-face encounter with the Holy Spirit of God. The prophet Samuel described it to Saul this way:

> Then the Spirit of the LORD will come upon you, and you will prophesy with them and be turned into another man.
>
> —1 SAMUEL 10:6

A MIGHTY WIND

Is it really possible that the Holy Spirit can totally change us? Absolutely. If the Lord could turn mud into man as He breathed the breath of life into him, imagine what He can do by breathing on us again! That is what happened at Pentecost.

> And suddenly there came a sound from heaven, as of a rushing mighty wind, and it filled the whole house where they were sitting.
>
> —ACTS 2:2

Those who gathered in the Upper Room on the day of Pentecost felt the breath of almighty God. And as it blew gently upon them, they were transformed.

When the Holy Spirit empowers your life, you can expect three things to happen:

1. The Lord will become very close to you.

2. Because of that relationship, your ultimate desire will be to walk in the ways of God.

3. You will be miraculously transformed into a new person.

I am convinced that the Holy Spirit, alive and present on the earth today, is the sign of the covenant God has made with us through the blood of His Son Jesus.

> In Him you also trusted, after you heard the word of truth, the gospel of your salvation; in whom also, having believed, you were sealed with the Holy Spirit of promise.
>
> —EPHESIANS 1:13

I have met many people who pray, "Lord, send the Holy Spirit upon my life! Fill me with Your power!" The Holy Spirit will come when we honor the death of Jesus Christ and His blood.

For example, in the Old Covenant when blood was offered,

God sent fire, and His glory descended. Do you remember what occurred at the dedication of Solomon's great temple?

> When Solomon had finished praying, fire came down from heaven and consumed the burnt offering and the sacrifices; and the glory of the LORD filled the temple.
>
> —2 CHRONICLES 7:1

What was the sign of the Holy Spirit? In the Old Testament it was often fire (Lev. 9:23–24; 1 Kings 18:38; 2 Chron. 7:1) representing God's all-consuming holiness.

John the Baptist also prophesied:

> I indeed baptize you with water; but One mightier than I is coming, whose sandal strap I am not worthy to loose. He will baptize you with the Holy Spirit and fire.
>
> —LUKE 3:16

After Jesus shed His blood at Calvary, the Holy Spirit came as fire again. The disciples were gathered together in Jerusalem, as Jesus had commanded:

> Then there appeared to them divided tongues, as of fire, and one sat upon each of them. And they were all filled with the Holy Spirit.
>
> —ACTS 2:3–4

God will fill your life with the fire and glory of His Holy Spirit when you come to Him through the blood.

Andrew Murray, a prolific Christian author who lived from 1828 to 1917, wrote about the relationship between Jesus' blood and the Holy Spirit in his book *The Power of the Blood.*

> Where the blood is honored in faith or preaching, there the Spirit works; and where He works He always leads souls to the blood.[2]

TOUCHED BY THE ANOINTING

The Word of God declares that it is the anointing of the Holy Spirit that enables us to serve God. God told Moses:

> You shall anoint them...that they may minister to Me as priests.
>
> —EXODUS 40:15

I learned years ago that without the anointing of the Holy Spirit upon my life, there is no ministry. I am always aware of the fact that what God is doing He is doing because of His anointing. Without it I would be spiritually bankrupt.

My daily prayer is "Lord, don't ever lift Your anointing from me." I know the danger that exists if that anointing should ever lift.

The life of Saul contains a great lesson. Saul had been chosen by God, and his life had been transformed. But the day came when he chose to break the sacrificial laws God had given the Israelites. Samuel told Saul:

> You have done foolishly. You have not kept the commandment of the LORD your God, which He commanded you. For now the LORD would have established your kingdom over Israel forever.
>
> —1 SAMUEL 13:13

Not only did the anointing leave King Saul, but something happened that was far worse.

> But the Spirit of the LORD departed from Saul, and an evil spirit from the LORD troubled him.
>
> —1 SAMUEL 16:14, KJV

The story of Samson provides another example of what can happen to a man when the anointing no longer rests upon his life. When the Holy Spirit left his life, he became a prisoner and a slave to the Philistines and lost his sight. He wasn't even aware that the anointing on his life had left, for the Bible states that he lost the anointing while he slept (Judg. 16:18–20).

I believe that sleeping here is symbolic of prayerlessness. As Samson slept, destruction came upon him. In a moment's time God's glory and presence left his life, and he became a captive of the Philistines. Only as he called upon God did his strength return. And as God's presence returned to his life and rested upon him once again, God used him to defeat the Philistines.

We must not neglect prayer or reject God's precious Word, lest we should lose His wonderful anointing on our lives.

When you and I pray, incredible things happen:

- Prayer produces spiritual strength. So you will have the strength to resist temptation and sin.

- Prayer produces beauty in your walk with God. It drives away the ugliness of sin and brings the beauty of righteousness to your life.

- Prayer draws you closer to God and separates you from the things of the world.

Although you are in the world, you will not be "of" the world. You and I are called to be awake and alert—vigilant watchmen in the kingdom. Jesus made it clear when He told us to "watch and pray" (Matt. 26:41).

The prophet Isaiah said, "Arise, shine; for your light has come! And the glory of the LORD is risen upon you" (Isa. 60:1).

There is nothing more I desire in this life than to have the anointing of the Holy Spirit rest upon my life. In fact, as I have said to the Lord so many times, "I would rather die than live one day without that precious anointing of the Holy Spirit resting upon me." And I believe that if you are reading this book, you too share that desire.

Until God's Spirit, the precious Holy Spirit, indwells us and fills us to overflowing, we merely exist. We begin to live when the blood of Jesus Christ cleanses us from all sin and the Holy Spirit breathes upon us. The Word declares, "I have come that they may have life, and that they may have it more abundantly" (John 10:10).

Remember that as you walk in obedience to God, you don't have to fear losing the anointing. You can look forward to God's blessings instead. That's what we'll see in the next step of the cleansing of the leper.

A COVENANT TO KEEP

1. Only after the blood of Jesus cleanses and sanctifies us can the Holy Spirit enter our lives. Remember, God is holy. As the temple of the Holy Spirit, our bodies must be cleansed and purified by the blood. Once the Holy Spirit begins working in your life, how does He minister to you? Read the following scriptures. Describe what each text says about the ministry of the Holy Spirit in your life.

The Word	The Work of the Holy Spirit
I Samuel 10:6	
Ezekiel 39:26–29	
Matthew 3:11	
John 14:15–31	
John 16:5–15	
Acts 1:7–8; 2:1–21	
I Corinthians 12:1–11	
Galatians 5:16–23	
Ephesians 5:18–19	
I John 3:24–4:10; 5:6–13	

2. Those who gathered in the Upper Room felt the breath of almighty God, and they were transformed. When the Holy Spirit empowers your life, you can expect three things to happen:

a. The Lord will become very close to you.

b. The Holy Spirit will come to dwell within you.

c. God's Spirit will breathe life into you.

What are some ways we can draw closer to God?

_____

_____

How does God fulfill His promises to us? (Read 2 Corinthians 1:20–22.)

_____

_____

3. Read Romans 15:13. What does the phrase "that you may overflow with hope by the power of the Holy Spirit" (NIV) mean to you?

_____

_____

Precious Jesus, thank You for shedding Your blood on the cross at Calvary. Thank You for Your supreme sacrifice and for cleansing me from all my sins. Transform me, daily, to become more like You, reflect Your image, and be a dwelling place of the Holy Spirit. In Your precious name I pray, amen.

Chapter 10

THERE'S
ANOINTING POWER
in the BLOOD

E VERY DAY IN prayer I thank God for the work of the cross and the blood of Jesus Christ. Because the blood was shed there for our sins, the Holy Spirit came, and today we can know and experience God's anointing on our lives and work.

When we are empowered by the oil of the Holy Spirit, we are freed from the chains of bondage. The prophet Isaiah wrote:

> It shall come to pass in that day that his burden will be taken away from your shoulder, and his yoke from your neck, and the yoke will be destroyed because of the anointing oil.
>
> —ISAIAH 10:27

Every time I am touched by the power of God, I feel like the psalmist who declared, "Let God arise, let His enemies be scattered" (Ps. 68:1).

Earlier we discovered how the blood brought cleansing to the leper, who symbolized sinful man. But that was only the beginning. Look what happened to the leper next. The blood made it possible for him to be anointed.

When a man was allowed back in the camp (Lev. 14:8), he was directed to "take two male lambs without blemish, one ewe lamb of the first year without blemish, three-tenths of an ephah of fine flour mixed with oil as a grain offering, and one log [about two-thirds of a pint] of oil" (Lev. 14:10).

The priest was to "take one male lamb and offer it as a trespass offering" (Lev. 14:12) as a restitution for a specific sin. "Then he shall kill the lamb in the place where he kills the sin offering and the burnt offering, in a holy place" (Lev. 14:13).

Did you notice that the man offered more sacrifices even after he was considered cleansed and allowed back into the camp?

In the same way, the Lord Jesus shed His blood once for the remission of our sins, but we continue to ask for the cleansing and protection that His blood provides. The Lord Jesus even taught His disciples to say in prayer:

> And forgive us our debts, as we forgive our debtors. And do not lead us into temptation, but deliver us from the evil one.
>
> —MATTHEW 6:12–13

The priest applied blood to the cleansed leper three times. After considerable study, I believe God had a specific purpose for each application of blood.

First, "the priest shall take some of the blood of the trespass offering, and the priest shall put it on the tip of the right ear" of the leper (Lev. 14:14).

When the blood is applied to our hearing, we are shielded from the voice of our enemies. The psalmist cried out to the Lord:

> Attend to me, and hear me; I am restless in my complaint, and moan noisily, because of the voice of the enemy, because of the oppression of the wicked; for they bring down trouble upon me, and in wrath they hate me.
>
> —PSALM 55:2–3

As believers we have power over verbal attacks of the enemy. The Bible says:

> No weapon formed against you shall prosper, and every tongue which rises against you in judgment you shall condemn. This is the heritage of the servants of the LORD.
>
> —ISAIAH 54:17

Whose tongues arise against us? The lying tongues of the Lord's enemies. But we can condemn those voices through the blood of Christ and the authority of His Word.

When someone tells me that the devil has been speaking to them, I remind them of the wonderful words of Jesus: "My sheep hear My voice, and I know them, and they follow Me" (John 10:27).

It's not the voice of Satan that we should be listening for but the voice of the Savior. That is why we need the blood applied to our hearing.

Second, the priest then reached out to the leper and placed the blood "on the thumb of his right hand" (Lev. 14:14).

Our hands represent the work that we do. It is wonderful to know that the Lord gives guidance and protection to our work. David said:

> And let the beauty of the LORD our God be upon us, and establish the work of our hands for us; yes, establish the work of our hands.
>
> —PSALM 90:17

And God told Isaiah:

> I will direct their work in truth, and will make with them an everlasting covenant.
>
> —ISAIAH 61:8

Finally, the priest applied blood to the leper "on the big toe of his right foot" (Lev. 14:14).

Our feet are symbolic of our daily walk with the Lord. "If we walk in the light as He is in the light, we have fellowship with one another, and the blood of Jesus Christ His Son cleanses us from all sin" (1 John 1:7).

SPRINKLED AND POURED

The application of the blood by the priest to the leper's ear, hand, and foot was first for cleansing, but it didn't stop there.

As you will recall from Leviticus 14, the leper was cleansed from leprosy as the blood was applied seven times, and then the blood was applied to his earlobe, his thumb, and his toe, symbolically speaking of his hearing, his work, and his walk.

The moment the blood was applied, the priest was instructed to take "some of the log of oil, and pour it into the palm of his own left hand. Then the priest shall dip his right finger in the oil that is in his left hand, and shall sprinkle some of the oil with his finger seven times before the LORD" (Lev. 14:15–16).

Wherever the blood was in the Old Covenant, the glory descended and consumed the sacrifice. For example, when Moses offered up the sacrifices, the Word of God says the fire descended and consumed the sacrifice. Whenever the blood was applied, the glory descended and the cloud filled the tabernacle.

If you want God to anoint you today, apply the blood afresh on your life.

The anointing oil throughout Scripture represents the work of the Holy Spirit in consecrating and empowering for service.

It is essential to understand that God anoints what the blood has covered. The anointing of the Holy Spirit follows the blood. The anointing oil was sprinkled seven times—God's number of completion—to represent the reception of a total anointing.

What took place next may sound repetitious, but God was doing something totally new. The priest took the oil and anointed the leper's right ear, right thumb, and right big toe once again.

The blood was already there, but the anointing oil was placed on top of it. For where you find the blood of the cross, you will find the anointing of the Holy Spirit.

I believe the anointing of the Holy Spirit multiplies and expands the benefits of the blood, enabling the believer to live an over-coming, victorious life.

- When the blood is applied to our hearing, we will not hear the enemy's voice; then God brings the anointing so we can hear His voice.

- When the blood is applied to our hands, the devil cannot touch our work for God; then the anointing multiplies our efforts.

- When the blood is applied to our walk, then God anoints our steps so that we can walk with Him.

Andrew Murray said:

God gives Christians the Holy Spirit with this intention, that every day all their life should be lived in the power of the Spirit. A man cannot live one hour a godly life unless by the power of the Holy Ghost. He may live a proper, consistent life, as people call it, an irreproachable life, a life of virtue and diligent service; but to live a life acceptable to God, in the enjoyment of God's salvation and God's love, to live and walk in the power of the new life—he cannot do it unless he be guided by the Holy Spirit every day and every hour....

The Father in Heaven loves to fill His children with His Holy Spirit. God longs to give each one individually, separately, the power of the Holy Spirit for daily life....

Are you living a life under the power of the Holy Spirit day by day, or are you attempting to live without that? Remember you cannot....And now are you willing to give yourselves up to the Holy Spirit? You can do it now. A great deal may still be dark and dim, and beyond what we understand, and you may feel nothing; but come. God alone can effect the change. God alone, who gave us the Holy Spirit, can restore the Holy Spirit in power into our life. God alone can "strengthen us with might by his Spirit in the inner man." And to every waiting heart that will make the sacrifice, and give up everything, and give time to cry and pray to God, the answer will come. The blessing is not far off. Our God delights to help us. He will enable us to perfect, not in the flesh, but in the Spirit, what was begun in the Spirit.[1]

Our walk also needs to be washed with God's Word. Jesus said:

> He who is bathed needs only to wash his feet.
>
> —JOHN 13:10

We have been redeemed and washed by the blood, but our walk needs to be cleansed by God's Word every day (Eph. 5:26). Why? Because our lives constantly touch the dirt of the world.

In the Old Covenant, when God told Moses to build the tabernacle, He gave him precise details regarding every aspect, including the clothing required for the priests. (See Exodus 39.) But they were given no instructions regarding shoes. To remind them that they were still touching the dust of the earth, they were to walk with bare feet.[2]

As Christians we are touching the world every day. That's why we need to come back to the Lord daily and say, "Cleanse me anew and wash me again."

HEAD TO TOE

What did God command the priest to do with the remaining oil?

> The rest of the oil that is in the priest's hand he shall put on the head of him who is to be cleansed. So the priest shall make atonement for him before the LORD.
>
> —LEVITICUS 14:18

God wants to cover us totally from head to toe with the oil of His Spirit—our thoughts, our sight, our words, and our entire lives.

Not only do we have the atonement of the blood, but we have the anointing of the Holy Spirit.

Many people, however, don't think they are good enough for God's anointing because of their past. Friend, let me tell you what the shed blood of Jesus does to your past.

A COVENANT TO KEEP

1. The Book of Psalms often speaks of "the Lord's anointed."
   While these verses point to the coming of our Messiah,
   Jesus Christ, they also speak of the blessings associated
   with the anointing of God. Read each verse and describe
   the blessings each verse gives for the believer who has
   access through Christ's blood and the indwelling Holy
   Spirit to the anointing of God.

Verse	Blessing of the Anointing
Psalm 15:5	
Psalm 20:6	
Psalm 45:7	
Psalm 84:9	
Psalm 92:10	
Psalm 105:15	
Psalm 132:17	

2. We have been redeemed and washed by the blood, but
   our walk needs to be cleansed by God's Word every day
   because our lives constantly touch the dirt of the world
   (Eph. 5:26). Examine your life. On the lines below, describe
   how the cleansing of the blood and the anointing of the
   Holy Spirit can help you in each of these three areas:

   My hearing (thought life, mind, and emotions)

   _____

   _____

My hands (work, career, and job)

_____

_____

My walk (spiritual disciplines, relationship with others and with the Lord)

_____

_____

Lord Jesus, cover me with Your precious blood, which cleanses me from sin. Holy Spirit, fill my life and prepare me to be a dwelling place for You, dear Lord. Father, cover me with the blood of Your own Son and grant me access to the blessings of heaven. Anoint me from the top of my head to the tip of my toes that I may be dedicated fully to You, wonderful Lord. Amen.

Chapter 11

THERE'S NEW LIFE
in the BLOOD

MILLIONS OF PEOPLE live in a never-ending cycle of hope-lessness and despair because they cannot forget about yesterday. They are tormented by memories that can lead to depression, mental anguish, and even thoughts of suicide.

Satan is aware of our weaknesses. That is why he uses our past mistakes to torture and trap us. One of the devil's greatest weapons against us is our past.

But when you understand the work of the cross and the power of the blood, those dead works will be removed from your conscience, "for it is the blood that makes atonement for the soul" (Lev. 17:11).

> For if the blood of bulls and of goats, and the ashes of an heifer sprinkling the unclean, sanctifieth to the purifying of the flesh: how much more shall the blood of Christ, who through the eternal Spirit offered himself without spot to God, purge your conscience from dead works to serve the living God?
>
> —HEBREWS 9:13–14, KJV

Do you realize how liberating it is to be freed from your past? Can you fully comprehend what it means to live without guilt or condemnation?

You may think your past is especially blemished compared to those around you. But R. A. Torrey says:

> If we could see our past as God sees it before it is washed, the record of the best of us would be black, black, black. But if we are walking in the light, submitting to the truth of God,

believing in the light, in Christ, our record today is [as] white
as Christ's garments were when the disciples saw Him on the
Mount of Transfiguration (Matt. 17:2; Luke 9:29; Mark 9:3).[1]

Let these words sink into your heart: The moment the shed
blood of Christ has been applied to your heart, your past is buried.
It is gone forever and no longer remembered in glory. To dwell on
it is an insult to God.

APPEARING IN COURT

Imagine yourself in a courtroom. God is the Judge, and you are
standing before Him. In the presence of His holiness, you are over-
whelmed by a relentless consciousness of your sin.

God's voice thunders out, "I know you are guilty."

You tremble before the holy and righteous Judge, knowing you
deserve the sentence of death. Then God continues, "You are guilty,
but I declare you righteous. Your punishment is waived."

That is called justification. God gives you a new legal standing.
Your slate is clean. God declares you righteous because of what
Jesus has done.

> God had passed over the sins that were previously committed,
> to demonstrate at the present time His righteousness, that He
> might be just and the justifier of the one who has faith in Jesus.
> —ROMANS 3:25–26

The shed blood of Jesus saves us from the wrath of a holy God
poured out against sin.

> Much more then, having now been justified by His blood, we
> shall be saved from wrath through Him.
> —ROMANS 5:9

R. A. Torrey makes a wonderful comparison between forgiveness
and justification:

In forgiveness we are stripped of the vile and stinking rags of our sins, in justification we are clothed upon with the glory and beauty of Christ.[2]

IF I WERE AN ANT

Have you ever walked along a road and stepped on an anthill? Billy Graham tells the story of a time many years ago when he went out for a walk with his young son and they came across an anthill. From the appearance of things, someone must have given the anthill a kick a bit earlier, either accidentally or on purpose, because all around the anthill there were dead and dying ants. In addition, there were ants scurrying around on the collapsed anthill looking completely lost.

"It was as though I, while walking along a road, stepped on an anthill," he said. "I might look down and say to the ants, 'I am terribly sorry that I've stepped on your anthill. I've disrupted your home. Everything is in confusion. I wish I could tell you that I care, that I did not mean to do it, that I would like to help you.'

"But you say, 'That's absurd; that's impossible. Ants cannot understand your language!' That's just it! How wonderful it would be if I could only become an ant for a few moments and in their own language tell them of my concern for them!

"That, in effect, is what Christ did. He came to reveal God to men. He it is who told us that God loves us and is interested in our lives. He it is who told us of the mercy and long-suffering and grace of God. He it is who promised life everlasting."[3]

To bridge the gap between God and man, Jesus humbled Himself and took the form of a man. He was fully God and fully man. To be the complete expression of God, He had to be God; to communicate and understand man, He had to be human as well.

A JUST AND LOVING GOD

Can God, who is perfect and holy, be just and still justify the sinner? If so, how is this accomplished?

The Word of God says:

> But God demonstrates His own love toward us, in that while we were still sinners, Christ died for us. Much more then, having now been justified by His blood, we shall be saved from wrath through Him. For if when we were enemies we were reconciled to God through the death of His Son, much more, having been reconciled, we shall be saved by His life. And not only that, but we also rejoice in God through our Lord Jesus Christ, through whom we have now received the reconciliation.
>
> —ROMANS 5:8–11

When you and I are justified by His blood, it means we are pronounced innocent or absolved of all guilt. Sin is not simply pardoned or excused; it is put away and made as though it had never been. Imagine the dimension of such perfect love and grace to allow man to be viewed as innocent and taken back to the position he occupied before he fell from grace, enjoying the kind of relationship Adam knew in the Garden of Eden. In order for God to be true to Himself in all His attributes while justifying the sinner, only one solution existed. That required an innocent volunteer to die physically and spiritually as a substitute for the guilty.

After the fall of man, no such individual existed on earth, for the Bible declares that "all have sinned" (Rom. 3:23). There was only One who could become man's substitute—Jesus, God's Son.

THREE ASPECTS OF THE CROSS

When we look at the cross of Christ, we see three things:

1. A description of the depth of man's sin. Neither the Roman soldiers nor people of that day were responsible for the crucifixion of our wonderful Lord. All of mankind, including you and me, are just as guilty, for it was your sins and my sins that made it necessary for Him to become the supreme sacrifice.

2. The overwhelming love of God. In the cross you find an immeasurable expression of God's love.

3. The only means or way of salvation is found in the cross.

Jesus said, "I am the way, the truth, and the life. No one comes to the Father except through Me" (John 14:6). There is no possibility of being saved from sin and hell except by identifying yourself with the Christ of the cross.

Maxwell Whyte offered these thoughts about the day Jesus was crucified in his book *The Power of the Blood*:

> Imagine, if you can, the scene at Calvary. No artist has ever pictured the Calvary scene as it really was. It would be too repulsive to paint on any canvas. It is doubtful that the Romans left Jesus even the courtesy of a loincloth. He became as the first Adam in the garden, that He might cover His own nakedness with His own precious Blood—not even a linen cloth to spoil the type. In turn, we may cover our nakedness with His precious Blood—a perfect atonement or covering indeed! We cannot even offer a convenient loincloth or fig leaf to hide our sins; we must divest ourselves of everything and appear destitute of all covering in His presence. Then He will give us His own blessed robe of righteousness after we have accepted the cleansing of His precious Blood. A glorious truth indeed!
>
> The crown of thorns was then put upon His head, not gently but roughly; many thorns (maybe a dozen or more),

one-and-a-half inches long, jabbed into His scalp, producing such serious wounds that trickles of Blood spurted out and ran into His hair and beard, matting both in dark red. The spikes were driven into the palms of His hands, and His Blood coursed down His arms and sides. (Later the spear was thrust into His side and His Blood spilled out and ran down the sides of the cross onto the ground beneath.) Spikes were also driven through His feet and more Blood ran down the sides of the cross on behalf of the sins of the whole world.

His bones were out of joint. (See Psalm 22.) His face was dreadful to look upon. There was no beauty in Him that we should desire Him (Isa. 53:2). God gave His best, His Son, His perfect sacrifice—and even in death, there was no blemish in Him, for He was already dead when the soldiers arrived to break His legs; therefore, not a bone of Him was broken. Those who looked on Him saw only Blood. It was a spectacle of blood. His hair and beard were soaked in His own Blood. His back was lacerated from the thirty-nine stripes and was covered with His own Blood. Even the cross was covered with Blood, and the very earth was soaked. Every type of the atonement was fulfilled in Christ. It was Blood, Blood, Blood.[4]

Scripture tells us, "He was oppressed and He was afflicted, yet He opened not His mouth; He was led as a lamb to the slaughter, and as a sheep before its shearers is silent, so He opened not His mouth" (Isa. 53:7).

THE BLOOD AND A CLEAR CONSCIENCE

The sins of your past cannot be erased simply because you want them to be. You cannot be freed from a sinful life by merely saying, "I'm going to forget about it."

God said He would "purge" us. The blood will purge your conscience completely—not only your transgressions, but also every thought connected with them.

Nothing but the blood of Christ can cleanse your mind from

thoughts of past and present sins. Since we have "a High Priest over the house of God, let us draw near with a true heart in full assurance of faith, having our hearts sprinkled from an evil conscience" (Heb. 10:21–22).

What is an evil conscience? One that remembers yesterday and whispers, "You're a sinner."

But in heaven the Lord says, "Welcome! I have delivered you from your iniquities. You are forgiven. Only saints can enter here, and the blood has made you righteous."

To many it sounds impossible that we can stand before God with the righteousness of Christ, but it is true. Because the blood of Jesus is pure, we become pure in God's sight. The Lord cleanses our minds from the past and the present. That is why I love to sing, "There is power, power, wonder-working power in the precious blood of the Lamb."[5]

Basilea Schlink, in her book titled *Repentance: The Joy-Filled Life*, reminds you and me of our need for a continuing attitude of repentance:

> We are apathetic and indifferent towards our sins, and we are usually not disturbed by them at all. We are more likely to weep over what is done to us, or over difficult leadings. We weep over our sorrows, troubles and disappointments. Each one of us does so, for this is our human nature. But not everyone comes to the point of true contrition and repentance and weeps over his sins. Such reactions are foreign to human nature. The human heart has a way of thinking it is always in the right and has no need to weep over its sins. By nature we are self-confident and impenitent. We blame others or even accuse God when we do not understand His ways.
>
> Repentance truly lets us experience the kingdom of heaven with all its blessings, for it brings us the most beautiful and most wonderful gift: an overflowing love for Jesus.
>
> Repentance is the way that leads us to this lavish, whole-hearted love for Jesus, bringing with it such a great treasure of

grace and blessing. We see this in the life of Mary Magdalene. She had nothing to bring to Jesus but her sin, for what had she done to God and man! Yet her life was so enriched by the deep love that repentance kindled in her. She became an example for us all.[6]

Because of God's promises you can say, "The blood has cleansed me of my sin and washed my past, and I am free!"

By His promise you can now say, "The blood has washed my past, and I am free!"

Satan will always attempt to torment you by asking, "But what about your past?"

As I often say, when Satan harasses you and tries to remind you of your past, remind him of his future!

As for you and me, we have reason to rejoice "in hope of the glory of God"!

> Therefore, having been justified by faith, we have peace with God through our Lord Jesus Christ, through whom also we have access by faith into this grace in which we stand, and rejoice in hope of the glory of God.
>
> —ROMANS 5:1–2

A COVENANT TO KEEP

"Confession is good for the soul," so the saying goes. The Word of God declares that when we confess our sins, God will forgive us of our sins and cleanse us from all unrighteousness (1 John 1:9). Many, however, insult the work of the cross and our wonderful Lord Jesus when they continually revisit the guilt of their past. Remember, the Holy Spirit convicts us of sin; the accuser wants us to feel guilty about sin so that he can render our lives and testimonies powerless to those who know us.

1. Think about your own life. On the lines below, list any unconfessed sin from the past about which you still feel guilt and pain.

   Confessed sin I still feel guilty about:

   _____

   _____

2. Using a concordance, write down Scripture verses that speak of God's love, forgiveness, and mercy. Commit a different verse to memory each day this week. As you do, release that guilt to the cleansing blood of Jesus Christ, and live in the forgiveness available to you through the mercy and love of God. This is how God sees your sin once the blood has been applied to your life. Pray and thank Jesus for His shed blood as you do this.

Psalm 51 is an important psalm of confession and forgiveness. As you read the psalm, write your name on each blank line. Announce to the enemy that you are forgiven. As you pray the words of this psalm, allow the cleansing blood of Jesus to wash you white as snow.

PRAYING PSALM 51

Have mercy upon (me) _____, O God, according to Your lovingkindness; according to the multitude of Your tender mercies, blot out my transgressions. Wash (me) _____ thoroughly from my iniquity, and cleanse me from my sin.

For I acknowledge my transgressions, and my sin is always before me. Against You, You only, [has] _____ sinned, and done this evil in Your sight—that You may be found just when You speak, and blameless when You judge.

Behold, (I) _____ was brought forth in iniquity; and in sin my mother conceived me. Behold, You desire truth in the inward parts, and in the hidden part You will make me to know wisdom.

Purge me with hyssop, and I shall be clean; wash me, and (I) _____ shall be whiter than snow. Make (me) _____ hear joy and gladness, that the bones You have broken may rejoice. Hide Your face from my sins, and blot out all my iniquities.

Create in (me) _____ a clean heart, O God, and renew a steadfast spirit within me. Do not cast (me) _____ away from Your presence, and do not take Your Holy Spirit from (me) _____.

Restore to (me) _____ the joy of Your salvation, and uphold (me) _____ by Your generous Spirit. Then (I) _____ will teach transgressors Your ways, and sinners shall be converted to You.

Deliver (me) _____ from the guilt of bloodshed, O God, the God of my salvation, and my tongue shall sing aloud of Your righteousness. O Lord, open my lips, and my mouth shall show forth Your praise. For You do not desire sacrifice, or else I would give it; You do not delight in burnt offering. The sacrifices of God are a broken spirit, a broken and a contrite heart—these, O God, You will not despise. Amen.

Chapter 12

THERE'S FREEDOM
in the BLOOD

URING THE YEARS when slavery was legal in the United States, a gentleman happened upon a slave-bidding in a crowded street.

The man paused to observe the activities. As he watched from the edge of the crowd, he saw one slave after another led onto a platform, their arms and legs shackled with ropes as if they were animals.

Displayed before the jeering crowd, they were auctioned off, one by one. Some onlookers would inspect the "merchandise," grabbing disrespectfully at the women and examining the muscular arms of the men.

The gentleman studied the group of slaves waiting nearby. He paused when he saw a young girl standing at the back. Her eyes were filled with fear; she looked so frightened. He hesitated for a moment and then disappeared briefly. When he returned, the auctioneer was about to start the bidding for the young girl he had noticed beforehand.

As the auctioneer opened the bidding, the gentleman shouted out a bid that was twice the amount of any other selling price offered that day. There was silence for an instance, and then the gavel fell as "Sold to the gentleman" was heard.

The gentleman stepped forward, making his way through the crowd. He waited at the bottom of the steps as the young girl was led down to her new owner. The rope that bound her was handed to the man, who accepted it without saying anything.

The young girl stared at the ground. Suddenly she looked up and

117

spit in his face. Silently, he reached for a handkerchief and wiped the spittle from his face. He smiled gently at the young girl and said, "Follow me."

She followed him reluctantly. As they reached the edge of the crowd, he continued to a nearby area where each deal was closed legally. When a slave was set free, legal documents, called "manumission papers," were necessary.

The gentleman paid the purchase price and signed the necessary documents. When the transaction was complete, he turned to the young girl and presented the documents to her. Startled, she looked at him with uncertainty. Her eyes asked, "What are you doing?"

The gentleman responded to her questioning look. He said, "Here, take these papers. I bought you to set you free. As long as you have these papers in your possession, no man can ever make you a slave again."

The girl looked into his face. What was happening? There was silence.

Slowly she said, "You bought me to set me free? You bought me to set me free?" As she repeated this phrase over and over, the significance of what had just happened became more and more real to her.

"You bought me to set me free?" Was it possible that a stranger had just granted her freedom and never again could she be held in bondage and servitude to any man? As she began to grasp the significance of the documents that she now held in her hand, she fell to her knees and wept at the gentleman's feet.

Through her tears of joy and gratitude she said, "You bought me to set me free? I'll serve you forever!"

You and I were once bound in slavery to sin. But the Lord Jesus paid the price to set us free when He shed His blood at Calvary. That's what the Bible calls redemption.

> In Him we have redemption through His blood, the forgiveness of sins, according to the riches of His grace.
> —EPHESIANS 1:7

That's what Paul was referring to when he wrote:

> For you were bought at a price; therefore glorify God in your
> body and in your spirit, which are God's.
>
> —1 CORINTHIANS 6:20

The blood of Jesus was not spilled; it was shed. It was no accident. The Lord chose to die in our place, shedding His precious blood on our behalf. Jesus said of Himself:

> The Son of Man did not come to be served, but to serve, and
> to give His life a ransom for many.
>
> —MATTHEW 20:28

Why did Christ redeem us? To ransom us from sin and reconcile us back to God so "that the body of sin might be done away with, that we should no longer be slaves of sin" (Rom. 6:6). That is the only way we could "be dead indeed to sin, but alive to God in Christ Jesus our Lord" (Rom. 6:11).

Christ's purpose for coming into the world was that He might offer His life as a sacrifice for the sins of men. He came to die. And because He willingly gave His life as the supreme sacrifice, we can rejoice—not only in what we have been redeemed from, but to what we have been redeemed. We have been set free from slavery to sin and Satan. And we have been redeemed to a new liberty from sin and to a new life in Christ (2 Cor. 3:17–18).

When you have been redeemed by His blood, you can say:

> I have been crucified with Christ; it is no longer I who live,
> but Christ lives in me; and the life which I now live in the
> flesh I live by faith in the Son of God, who loved me and gave
> Himself for me.
>
> —GALATIANS 2:20

RECONCILED BY THE BLOOD

Who was most in need in the story at the beginning of this chapter, the slave girl or the man who bought her? The slave girl, of course. In the same way, God did not need to be reconciled to man; man needed to be reconciled to God.

> For it pleased the Father that in Him all the fullness should dwell, and by Him to reconcile all things to Himself, by Him, whether things on earth or things in heaven, having made peace through the blood of His cross. And you, who once were alienated and enemies in your mind by wicked works, yet now He has reconciled in the body of His flesh through death, to present you holy, and blameless, and above reproach in His sight.
>
> —COLOSSIANS 1:19–22

When the slave girl understood the full significance of the man's selfless expression of compassion, she fell at his feet in gratitude and promised to serve him for the rest of her life.

Your salvation was the most expensive thing in the universe, for it cost our heavenly Father His only begotten Son, Jesus Christ. I believe when you and I understand how great a price was paid so we could be liberated from the bondage of sin, like the slave girl we will fall at the feet of our Master, our wonderful Lord Jesus, and commit our lives in service to Him forever.

RECONCILIATION AND RELATIONSHIP

There was once a Shakespearean actor who was known everywhere for his one-man show of readings and recitations from the classics. He would always end his performance with a dramatic reading of Psalm 23. Each night, without exception, as the actor began his recitation—"The Lord is my Shepherd. I shall not want"—the crowd would listen attentively. And then, at the conclusion of the psalm, they would rise in thunderous applause in appreciation of the actor's incredible ability to bring the verse to life.

But one night, just before the actor was to offer his customary recital of Psalm 23, a young man from the audience spoke up.

"Sir, do you mind if tonight I recite Psalm 23?"

The actor was quite taken aback by this unusual request, but he allowed the young man to come forward and stand front and center on the stage to recite the psalm, knowing that the ability of this unskilled youth would be no match for his own talent.

With a soft voice, the young man began to recite the words of the psalm. When he was finished, there was no applause. There was no standing ovation as on other nights. All that could be heard was the sound of weeping. The audience had been so moved by the young man's recitation that every eye was full of tears.

Amazed by what he had heard, the actor said to the youth, "I don't understand. I have been performing Psalm 23 for years. I have a lifetime of experience and training, but I have never been able to move an audience as you have tonight. Tell me, what is your secret?"

The young man humbly replied, "Well, sir, you know the psalm… but I know the Shepherd."

The dimension of God's love is beyond comprehension. The Bible declares:

> Moreover the law entered that the offense might abound. But where sin abounded, grace abounded much more.
>
> —ROMANS 5:20

In the early 1900s, Frederick M. Lehman penned the words to a beautiful hymn titled "The Love of God." The moving lyrics almost present a sermon as they vividly describe God's eternal love and, in my opinion, furnish only a glimpse of His immeasurable and unending love for mankind.

The love of God is greater far than tongue or pen can ever
tell;

It goes beyond the highest star and reaches to the lowest hell;

The guilty pair, bowed down with care, God gave His Son to
win;

His erring child He reconciled, and pardoned from his sin.

When hoary time shall pass away and earthly thrones and
kingdoms fall;

When men, who here refuse to pray, on rocks and hills and
mountains call;

God's love so sure shall still endure, all measureless and
strong;

Redeeming grace to Adam's race—the saints' and angels'
song.

Could we with ink the ocean fill, and were the skies of
parchment made,

Were ev'ry stalk on earth a quill, and ev'ry man a scribe by
trade;

To write the love of God above would drain the ocean dry;

Nor could the scroll contain the whole, tho' stretched from
sky to sky.

O love of God, how rich and pure! How measureless and
strong!

It shall forevermore endure, the saints' and angels' song.[1]

Andrew Murray brings incredible insight to this subject in his book *The Power of the Blood*:

> Sin has had a twofold effect. It has had an effect on God as well as on man. But the effect it has exercised on God is more terrible and serious! It is because of its effect on God that sin has its power over us. God, as Lord of all, could not overlook sin. It is His unalterable law that sin must bring forth sorrow and death [Rom. 6:23].[2]

In the Old Covenant, God instructed His people to offer sacrifices. These slain animals symbolically bore the punishment for sin that the people deserved. But the sacrifices had to be made over and over.

The Old Covenant was the shadow (Heb. 10:1). The New Covenant brought the reality. Christ died "once for all," atoning for our sins and bringing us back into fellowship with God (Heb. 10:10). Righteousness demanded it; love offered it.

Now the Lord gives us a new responsibility: to share the message of reconciliation with the world.

> Now all things are of God, who has reconciled us to Himself through Jesus Christ, and has given us the ministry of reconciliation, that is, that God was in Christ reconciling the world to Himself, not imputing their trespasses to them, and has committed to us the word of reconciliation.
>
> —2 Corinthians 5:18–19

In the time of Christ, Gentiles were excluded from the family of God because they were not part of the old covenant. They were known as "aliens from the commonwealth of Israel and strangers from the covenants of promise, having no hope and without God in the world" (Eph. 2:12).

But through "the blood of Christ" these two groups—the Jews and the Gentiles—were made one, and He "has broken down the middle wall of separation" so "that He might reconcile them both to God in one body through the cross, thereby putting to death the enmity" (Eph. 2:13–14, 16). He made the Gentiles "fellow citizens with the saints and members of the household of God" (Eph. 2:19).

Removing the walls of hostility between people and between God and people is a part of Christ's great work as Mediator of the new covenant. That's a topic we will discuss in depth in the next chapter.

A Covenant to Keep

1. We have been redeemed from sin, bondage, and death. Recall your own personal redemption from sin.
   When did it happen?

   _____

   _____

   What was your heart condition at the time?

   _____

   _____

   What were the sins for which you needed God's redemption?

   _____

   _____

   How did you feel when you realized that because of the blood of Jesus, forgiveness had been applied to your life?

   _____

   _____

2. Not only does the shed blood of Jesus Christ release us from sin, bondage, and death; we are also redeemed to abundant life, freedom, and eternal life. The Bible is filled with the benefits of what you have been redeemed to in your new life in Christ. Read each passage listed below and describe what you discover.

The Bible	The Benefit
John 3:16	
John 10:10	
Romans 6:23	
Romans 10:9	
Romans 15:13	
Philippians 1:9–11	
Galatians 5:22–23	
1 John 2:25	

3. Reconciliation through the blood of Christ begins with your relationship with Jesus. But it doesn't end there. It's not enough for you to be reconciled. You must take the good news to others. Read the Great Commission of Jesus Christ. (See Matthew 28:18–20.) On the lines below, write down what you are doing to fulfill that commission.

_____

_____

Heavenly Father, I am forever grateful to You for the gift of salvation that You have given me. Jesus, thank You for shedding Your redeeming blood at Calvary. May I never take it for granted. Holy Spirit, I invite you to come and empower me to fulfill the Great Commission. Give me the boldness and courage I need to share the good news of Jesus with others. Amen.

Chapter 13

OUR MEDIATOR

I WATCHED IN AMAZEMENT in the fall of 1993 as the State of Israel and the Palestinian Liberation Organization (PLO) signed an agreement that laid a framework for peace between people whose hostilities ran decades and centuries deep.

Did those two powerful leaders just happen to meet one weekend? No. That historic moment came after years of negotiating through a third party—a mediator.

Because of His shed blood, the Lord Jesus has become our Mediator with the Father.

> And for this reason He is the Mediator of the new covenant, by means of death, for the redemption of the transgressions under the first covenant, that those who are called may receive the promise of the eternal inheritance.
> —HEBREWS 9:15

Mankind has always needed a mediator. Job declared, "Oh, that one might plead for a man with God" (Job 16:21).

Under the old covenant, the high priest became the legal representative of the people regarding spiritual matters. But there were some issues that he could not arbitrate. Eli, when he was the high priest of Israel, said:

> If one man sins against another, God will judge him. But if a man sins against the LORD, who will intercede for him?
> —1 SAMUEL 2:25

Today, Christ has become our High Priest through shedding His blood. That is what gives Him the authority to be our legal Mediator in heaven, representing us before the Father. Because of the cross, "He is the Mediator of the new covenant, by means of death, for the redemption of the transgressions under the first covenant" (Heb. 9:15).

As our Mediator, Christ intercedes on our behalf. The apostle Paul wrote, "It is Christ who died, and furthermore is also risen, who is even at the right hand of God, who also makes intercession for us" (Rom. 8:34). The Greek word for *intercession* is *entugchano*, which means to meet with and to make petition.

And because Christ is our High Priest, sin will not defeat us—no, not on a single score. He is our High Priest, ever living to make intercession for us.

> Therefore He is also able to save to the uttermost those who come to God through Him, since He always lives to make intercession for them.
>
> —HEBREWS 7:25

There is only one reason why Christ can be our go-between in heaven: because He is both God and man.

> And being found in appearance as a man, He humbled Himself and became obedient to the point of death, even the death of the cross.
>
> —PHILIPPIANS 2:8

> Inasmuch then as the children have partaken of flesh and blood, He Himself likewise shared in the same.
>
> —HEBREWS 2:14

Only Christ can say, "I know what man is like, and I can tell you what God is like. I understand them both from the inside out." When we are being tempted, Jesus can speak to the Father and say, "I went through the same thing."

He was sinless, and yet He became our sin bearer. Instead of symbolically cleansing us from defilement, the Lord cleansed us from actual sin. It was through the blood of the cross that the Lord Jesus removed the obstacle that had caused an estrangement between God and man and restored our fellowship with the Father.

> For we do not have a High Priest who cannot sympathize with our weaknesses, but was in all points tempted as we are, yet without sin.
> —HEBREWS 4:15

Though Christ is "holy, harmless, undefiled, separate from sinners, and has become higher than the heavens" (Heb. 7:26), He is nevertheless "touched with the feeling of our infirmities" (Heb. 4:15, KJV).

As the writer of Hebrews says, "Let us therefore come boldly" today to His "throne of grace, that we may obtain mercy" (Heb. 4:16). This wonderful Savior does not condemn you. He loves you, and He died for you.

> For there is one God and one Mediator between God and men, the Man Christ Jesus, who gave Himself a ransom for all.
> —1 TIMOTHY 2:5–6

And because of this ransom, God declares that we are free from the pit of sin and death.

> If there is a messenger for him, a mediator, one among a thousand, to show man His uprightness, then He is gracious to him, and says, "Deliver him from going down to the Pit; I have found a ransom."
> —JOB 33:23–24

So come to Jesus Christ our Mediator today. Jesus said, "I am the way, the truth, and the life. No one comes to the Father except through Me" (John 14:6).

PLEADING OUR CASES

We know that Christ is our Mediator, but He does even more for us. In that role He is also our Advocate, pleading and upholding our cases before the Father.

> My little children, these things I write to you, so that you may not sin. And if anyone sins, we have an Advocate with the Father, Jesus Christ the righteous.
>
> —1 JOHN 2:1

Because of the unrelenting temptation of Satan, many Christians find themselves out of fellowship with the Father. That is when they need someone who will speak on their behalf.

Jesus does not plead the case of sinners. It is only when the blood has been applied to our hearts that the Lord becomes our Advocate. It is then we can say, "The LORD is my helper; I will not fear" (Heb. 13:6).

BOLDNESS BY THE SHED BLOOD

Because the Lord Jesus sits at the right hand of the Father, we can enter boldly into the throne room.

> Therefore, brethren, having boldness to enter the Holiest by the blood of Jesus, by a new and living way which He consecrated for us, through the veil, that is, His flesh, and having a High Priest over the house of God, let us draw near with a true heart in full assurance of faith, having our hearts sprinkled from an evil conscience and our bodies washed with pure water.
>
> —HEBREWS 10:19–22

Our boldness to enter comes only because of Christ's sacrifice, nothing else. If we are still in our sin, no amount of brazen courage will open heaven's gates. Entrance is gained only through the shed blood of Jesus Christ and its power over sin.

If you long to experience the power of redemption that Jesus accomplished, notice what the passage from Hebrews 10:19–20 says about the holy of holies, which is now open to us, and the freedom with which we can enter through the shed blood of Christ.

These verses say that God has prepared four things for us:

- "The Holiest" or most holy place—the place where God dwells or resides
- The blood of Jesus
- A new and living way
- A High Priest

In response, we are to "draw near" with the following:

- A true heart
- Full assurance of faith
- Hearts sprinkled from an evil conscience
- Bodies washed with pure water

The shed blood of Christ has removed any need for us to be timid about approaching the Lord. The Word says:

> Let us therefore come boldly to the throne of grace, that we may obtain mercy and find grace to help in time of need.
> —HEBREWS 4:16

The shed blood of Christ gives us the confidence not only to approach His throne but also to reach the lost.

After Christ returned to glory, the disciples went everywhere preaching the message of the cross. They proclaimed it without fear and were undaunted when they were cross-examined by priests at the temple in Jerusalem.

Now when they saw the boldness of Peter and John, and perceived that they were uneducated and untrained men, they marveled. And they realized that they had been with Jesus.

—ACTS 4:13

At the newly formed church in Jerusalem, the Christians prayed for the disciples with these words:

Lord...grant to Your servants that with all boldness they may speak Your word, by stretching out Your hand to heal, and that signs and wonders may be done through the name of Your holy Servant Jesus.

—ACTS 4:29–30

Their prayer was answered. "The place where they were assembled together was shaken; and they were all filled with the Holy Spirit, and they spoke the word of God with boldness" (Acts 4:31).

So go ahead and become bold in your faith. "The wicked flee when no one pursues, but the righteous are bold as a lion" (Prov. 28:1).

"WHO WILL TAKE THE SON?"

A wealthy man and his son loved to collect rare works of art. They would often sit together and admire the great works of art.

When the Vietnamese conflict broke out, the son went to war. He was very courageous and died in battle while rescuing another soldier. The father was notified, and he grieved deeply for his only son.

About a month later, just before Christmas, there was a knock at the door. A young man stood at the door with a large package in his hands. He said, "Sir, you don't know me, but I am the soldier for whom your son gave his life. He saved many lives that day, and he was carrying me to safety when a bullet struck him in the heart. He died instantly. He often talked about you and your love for art."

The young man held out his package. "I know this isn't much.

I'm not really a great artist, but I think your son would have wanted you to have this."

The father opened the package. It was a portrait of his son, painted by the young man. He stared in awe at the way the soldier had captured the personality of his son in the painting. The father was so drawn to the eyes that his own eyes welled up with tears. He thanked the young man and offered to pay him for the picture.

"Oh no, sir, I could never repay what your son did for me. It's a gift."

The father hung the portrait over his mantle. Every time visitors came to his home he took them to see the portrait of his son before he showed them any of the other great works he had collected.

The man died a few months later. Because his only son was dead, there was to be a great auction to dispose of his paintings. Many influential people gathered, excited over seeing the great paintings and having an opportunity to purchase some for their collections.

On the platform sat the painting of the son. The auctioneer pounded his gavel. "We will start the bidding with this picture of the son. Who will bid for this picture?"

There was silence. Then a voice in the back of the room shouted, "We want to see the famous paintings. Skip this one."

But the auctioneer persisted. "Will someone bid for this painting? Who will start the bidding? $100, $200?"

Another voice shouted angrily, "We didn't come to see this painting. We came to see the Van Goghs, the Rembrandts. Get on with the real bids!"

But still the auctioneer continued. "The son! The son! Who'll take the son?"

Finally, a voice came from the very back of the room. It was the longtime gardener of the man and his son. "I'll give $10 for the painting." Being a poor man, it was all he could afford.

"We have $10, who will bid $20?" the auctioneer asked.

"Give it to him for $10. Let's see the masters."

"Ten dollars is the bid; won't someone bid $20?"

The crowd was becoming angry. They didn't want the picture

of the son. They wanted the more worthy investments for their collections.

The auctioneer pounded the gavel. "Going once, twice, sold for $10!"

A man sitting on the second row shouted, "Now let's get on with the collection!"

The auctioneer laid down his gavel and said, "I'm sorry, sir, the auction is over."

"What about all the other paintings?"

"I am sorry. When I was called to conduct this auction, I was told of a secret stipulation in the will. I was not allowed to reveal that stipulation until this time. Only the painting of the son was to be auctioned. Whoever bought that painting would inherit the entire estate, including the paintings. The man who took the son gets everything!"

God gave His Son two thousand years ago to die on a cruel cross. Much like the auctioneer, His message today is, "The Son, the Son, who'll take the Son?" Because, you see, whoever takes the Son gets everything.

ETERNAL INHERITANCE

Christ shed His blood and became the Mediator of the new covenant so "those who are called may receive the promise of the eternal inheritance" (Heb. 9:15).

What God promised isn't just for today; it is for eternity. That's why it is an eternal inheritance.

The writer of Hebrews compares the new covenant to a last will and testament:

> For where there is a testament, there must also of necessity be the death of the testator. For a testament is in force after men are dead, since it has no power at all while the testator lives.
> —HEBREWS 9:16–17

In other words, the death of Jesus Christ activated the power of the blood that guaranteed our inheritance.

Some people have the idea that when we enter the kingdom of God, the Lord is going to judge us according to how we have lived, give us a mansion of gold, and that's it. No. The Bible says our inheritance is eternal, meaning it's an ongoing possession. When one reward is presented, I believe there will be another. From the perspective of a child, it would be like a Christmas that never ends.

Scripture tells us that "eye has not seen, nor ear heard, nor have entered into the heart of man the things which God has prepared for those who love Him" (1 Cor. 2:9). Peter says it is "an inheritance incorruptible and undefiled and that does not fade away, reserved in heaven for you" (1 Pet. 1:4).

The promises of God's Word—both the Old and New Testaments—are ours when we are redeemed by the blood.

> And if you are Christ's, then you are Abraham's seed, and heirs according to the promise.
>
> —GALATIANS 3:29

We don't deserve an inheritance because of our works of righteousness, "but according to His mercy He saved us...that having been justified by His grace we should become heirs according to the hope of eternal life" (Titus 3:5, 7).

Too many people fear that they'll never see their inheritance. That must be because they don't understand God's amazing grace.

> But as it is written: "Eye has not seen, nor ear heard, nor have entered into the heart of man the things which God has prepared for those who love Him."
>
> —1 CORINTHIANS 2:9

A COVENANT TO KEEP

1. Read Hebrews 6:19–20 and Hebrews 7. Not much is known about the high priest Melchizedek except the following:

   - There is no record of his birth, death, or genealogy.

   - His name means "king of righteousness," and as the king of Salem, his name means "king of peace."

   - He remains a priest forever.

   Christ, our Mediator, came as our High Priest in the order of Melchizedek, but Christ brought a greater covenant. Review the Scripture references above. In what ways is Christ the Supreme High Priest?

   _____

   _____

   How is His priesthood better than the Levitical priesthood?

   _____

   _____

2. The password into God's throne room is "I come by the blood." The moment you speak those words, entrance is yours. Before the sacrifice of Christ, only the high priest could enter the holy of holies to meet with God. But Christ's redemptive plan swung open the door into the very presence of God. Because of the power of redemption that Jesus accomplished, we can enter the holy of holies.

Read Hebrews 10:19–22. These verses tell us that God has prepared four things for us:

1. The Holiest, or most holy place—the place where God dwells

2. The blood of Jesus

3. A new and living way

4. A High Priest

In response, we are to "draw near" with the following:

1. A true heart

2. Full assurance of faith

3. Hearts sprinkled from an evil conscience

4. Bodies washed with pure water

Look over these two lists from Hebrews 10:19–22 one more time. Describe the one thing about approaching the throne of God for which you are most thankful.

_____

_____

Why is that the item you chose?

_____

_____

Praise Jesus for that one thing. Approach God's throne boldly!

Chapter 14

THERE'S REST
in the BLOOD

I N 1975 I was ministering at a conference in Brockville, Ontario. A number of ministers were scheduled to take part in the conference. Among them was David du Plessis, a dynamic speaker known as "Mr. Pentecost."

I had the privilege of meeting him for the first time while riding back to our hotel after a meeting. I hadn't been in the ministry very long, and I was thrilled to have this opportunity to meet him face to face.

David was a very dignified, quiet man who always carried his briefcase with him wherever he went. When we arrived at the hotel, he picked up his briefcase, got out of the car, and made his way into the hotel. I quickly got out of the car and hurried after him.

Moments later the elevator door opened, and we both got on the elevator to go to our rooms. As the elevator door closed, I'm certain that the excitement I felt was evident. He was so dignified and proper, while the excitement I felt made it almost impossible to stand still. I could hardly believe it. Here I was, all alone with this great giant of the faith and with a whole list of questions that I wanted to ask.

I took a deep breath and respectfully said, "Mr. Pentecost, may I ask you a question? I want to please God so much. Please tell me—how can I please God?"

David didn't respond but remained very quiet. About that time, the elevator stopped, and we stepped out and started walking down the hallway. Suddenly he stopped and put his briefcase down as he stuck his finger in my chest, pushing me up against a wall. He

138

looked at me with piercing eyes and said, "Don't even try. It's not your ability. It's His in you."

I will never forget that moment as long as I live. I just stood there, motionless, pondering his powerful words.

Then David said, "Good night," as he picked up his briefcase and walked away. I just stood there watching him as he disappeared down the hall and into his hotel room. Later, he would become a very dear friend to me and a great influence on my life.

RULES AND REGULATIONS

For some reason, people are drawn to works. I don't understand why, but it is true.

Some false religions call for a ritual of prayer five times a day. Others tell followers to purify themselves in the waters of sacred rivers or present gifts to gold-encrusted shrines. The world says, "Work! Work! Work!"

Some denominations began with an outpouring of the Holy Spirit and the love of God. Before long, however, the leaders added works. Legalism replaced the presence of the Holy Spirit.

The people in these churches were told, "Here is what it takes to get to heaven. If you follow these rules, you will keep your salvation, but if not, you will suffer the consequences." And they were given a one-two-three list of outward acts to perform. They followed the rules and regulations they were given because, by our very nature, human beings love works. We mistakenly believe that it is by actions that God is pleased.

When I became a Christian, I was surprised to find how many in the church were bound to rituals and spiritual protocol. A dear sister once sat me down and said, "Young man, do you know it's a sin to have long hair?" And she told me exactly how God wanted me to cut my shoulder-length hair.

Many people equate holiness with a pious outward appearance, but it is primarily a work of the heart. When we have been transformed from within, then we can demonstrate a consistently changed and transformed life.

It takes some people a lifetime to realize that holiness is not produced by legalism. Legalism is of the flesh, and God has no desire for it. Instead, "right living" is the result of our response to the grace of almighty God.

It's Not Your Ability

One day a man was driving his new pickup truck on a dusty New Mexico highway when he spotted a hitchhiker standing on the side of the road. The hitchhiker was carrying a large, heavy bag over his shoulder and looked exhausted in the heat of the day.

The driver stopped and asked, "Where are you headed?"

"Albuquerque," the man answered.

"Hop in the back, and I'll take you there," he said.

A few miles down the road the driver glanced in his rearview mirror and was surprised to see the man sitting in the bed of the truck with his bag over his shoulder. Why, he wondered, didn't he just put it down?

Finally, he stopped his little pickup, walked back to the man, and inquired, "Why don't you rest and put that bag down?"

"Oh," said the hitchhiker, "I don't want to hurt your new truck."

I have met many Christians who are a carbon copy of that man. They have the wheels of salvation beneath them, but they are still carrying their own heavy load.

Again and again Jesus says, "Put it down. I'll carry it for you."

Instead, they are proud of their self-effort and say, "No, Lord. I'd rather do it my own way."

How can they believe that they have been redeemed by the blood if they are trying to win heaven by their deeds?

After I met the Holy Spirit as a young man in Toronto, I spent many hours (sometimes up to eight hours a day) praying and fellowshipping with the Lord and studying His Word. One day I read a book about Martin Luther and how the Lord used him to bring the message of justification by faith to the church of his day. One portion of the book focused on Galatians, where Paul talks about how to be free from the curse of the law.

After reading that portion, I heard the Lord's voice say in my spirit, "Did you save yourself? Or was it My blood that saved you?"

"You saved me," I answered.

"Did you choose Me?" He asked.

"No, Lord. You chose me."

"Did you convict yourself of sin?"

"No. You convicted me of sin."

"Did you draw yourself to the cross?"

"No, Lord. You drew me to the cross."

At that moment I realized there is nothing I can do to merit God's grace and favor. It is not by any talent or ability I may possess but by Christ's blood and grace that the work is accomplished.

Mercy and grace were described in such an eloquent and profound way by Charles Spurgeon when he said, "Mercy and Grace are for the sinful, for none others need them; and God's Grace comes to us when we are far off by wicked works....Free Grace breaks forth like a mighty flood and sweeps in torrents over the hills of our transgressions, rising above the high alps of our presumptuous sins. Twenty cubits upward does this sea of Grace prevail till the tops of the mountains of iniquity are covered."[1]

No matter how many times a man says, "I've got to do it myself," when we see ourselves in the light of God's mercy and grace as described by Charles Spurgeon, we realize that in our strength we are miserable failures. It is only as we surrender completely and say, "I can't do it!" that we have taken the first step toward abundant life.

It seems we all have something in us that says, "I've got to do it myself." Perhaps it is to prove something. But again and again we realize that in our own strength we are miserable failures. It is when we finally surrender and say, "I can't do it!" that we have taken the first step to real living.

You may be struggling and agonizing over living the Christian life. Perhaps you are trying to please God and feel as if you're getting nowhere. As Kathryn Kuhlman often said, "Quit trying and surrender." That's all God asks you to do.

GRACE THAT'S AMAZING

In his letter to the church at Ephesus, Paul explains how we receive the amazing grace of God. He starts by describing where we were before we came under grace and still followed the ways of the world. We "were dead in trespasses and sins" (Eph. 2:1) and gratified the cravings of our sinful nature, "fulfilling the desires of the flesh and of the mind, and were by nature children of wrath" (Eph. 2:3).

Because of God's great mercy and love for us, "even when we were dead in trespasses, [He] made us alive together with Christ... and raised us up together, and made us sit together in the heavenly places in Christ Jesus" (Eph. 2:5–6).

Heaven will be ours—not because of what we have done but because of "the exceeding riches of His grace in His kindness toward us in Christ Jesus. For by grace you have been saved through faith, and that not of yourselves; it is the gift of God, not of works, lest anyone should boast" (Eph. 2:7–9).

The blood of Christ covers our sin, and we receive forgiveness through faith because of the grace of God. It is a message that every believer needs to understand.

Oswald Chambers states in his book *My Utmost for His Highest*:

> I am not saved by believing—I simply realize I am saved by believing. And it is not repentance that saved me—repentance is only the sign that I realize what God has done through Christ Jesus. The danger here is putting the emphasis on the effect, instead of on the cause. Is it my obedience, consecration, and dedication that make me right with God? It is never that! I am made right with God because, prior to all of that, Christ died. When I turn to God and by belief accept what

God reveals, the miraculous atonement by the Cross of Christ instantly places me into a right relationship with God. And as a result of the supernatural miracle of God's grace I stand justified, not because I am sorry for my sin, or because I have repented, but because of what Jesus has done. The Spirit of God brings justification with a shattering, radiant light, and I know that I am saved, even though I don't know how it was accomplished.

The salvation that comes from God is not based on human logic, but on the sacrificial death of Jesus. We can be born again solely because of the atonement of our Lord. Sinful men and women can be changed into new creations, not through their repentance or their belief, but through the wonderful work of God in Christ Jesus which preceded all of our experience. (See 2 Corinthians 5:17–19.)

The unconquerable safety of justification and sanctification is God Himself. We do not have to accomplish these things ourselves—they have been accomplished through the atonement of the Cross of Christ. The supernatural becomes natural to us through the miracle of God, and there is the realization of what Jesus Christ has already done—"It is finished!" (John 19:30).[2]

Religion says, "Do." Jesus says, "Done."

When Jesus shed His blood on the cross, He didn't say, "To be continued." He said, "It is finished" (John 19:30). The Bible declares that He is "the First and the Last" (Rev. 1:17) and "the author and finisher of our faith" (Heb. 12:2).

Because of the blood of the cross, "you are not under law but under grace" (Rom. 6:14). Your past was erased. You are free from guilt and have victory over Satan.

The Lord has provided you with "a better covenant, which was established on better promises" (Heb. 8:6). You are delivered from guilt and condemnation because the blood of Jesus Christ has been shed for your freedom and liberty (Rom. 6:18; Gal. 5:1). It's yours through God's grace.

FEAR AND FAITH

Many Christians today have the wrong picture of God.

From their childhood they have built an image of an almighty God who is harsh and austere—with glaring eyes of steel. They see Him with a whip in His hand, ready to beat them every time they make the slightest mistake.

But God is nothing like that. Though He occasionally chastises us for our good, He is always gentle, kind, and loving to His children.

I love the words of the great hymn "Praise, My Soul, the King of Heaven":

> Fatherlike, He tends and spares us;
> Well our feeble frame He knows.
> In His hands He gently bears us,
> Rescues us from all our foes.[3]

In that same hymn the writer says He's "slow to chide, and swift to bless." That's just what Psalm 103:8 says:

> The LORD is merciful and gracious, slow to anger, and abounding in mercy.

Those who continually approach the Lord and say, "I'm filthy. I'm a failure," do not know what the grace of God is all about. When you are bound by law, the entire focus of your life is sin. Yes, we need to confess our sins to Christ and ask for forgiveness, but there is a great difference between coming before Him with fear and entering His presence with confidence.

Beneath our confession there needs to be a tremendous faith that what Christ did at Calvary was not for our judgment but for our freedom. Stop looking at your failures and see God's mercy. He doesn't want to cast you aside but desires to hold you in His arms and say, "I love you."

For more than twelve hundred years the children of Israel followed rituals and sacrifices to atone for their sin. But their focus turned from the Lawgiver to the law, and they fell into bondage.

God repeatedly tried to call them back. He was saying, "What matters is your hearts—not your works. I want you to love Me; then you will obey Me."

You may say, "I thought the Old Testament dealt only with the law, not love."

It doesn't. Moses told the Israelites:

> Therefore you shall love the LORD your God, and keep His charge, His statutes, His judgments, and His commandments always.
>
> —DEUTERONOMY 11:1

God gave Israel a condition to His promise that the land would be fruitful for them. This condition was based on love—not works.

> And it shall be that if you earnestly obey My commandments which I command you today, to love the LORD your God and serve Him with all your heart and with all your soul, then I will give you the rain for your land in its season, the early rain and the latter rain, that you may gather in your grain, your new wine, and your oil. And I will send grass in your fields for your livestock, that you may eat and be filled.
>
> —DEUTERONOMY 11:13–15

God focused on love, not the law, because it wasn't just difficult for the children of Israel to obey the law; it was impossible. For the Scriptures state:

> A man is not justified by the works of the law but by faith in Jesus Christ...for by the works of the law no flesh shall be justified.
>
> —GALATIANS 2:16

It is impossible to obey God with our own strength. As my father-in-law, Roy Harthern, used to say, "Living the Christian life isn't difficult; it's impossible." But God sent the Holy Spirit to live in our hearts and enable us to obey His commands. God told His people through Ezekiel, "I will put My Spirit within you and cause you to walk in My statutes, and you will keep My judgments and do them" (Ezek. 36:27).

Even the early believers had to learn the fact that we are not justified by works but by faith in God. In Acts 15:1 the story is told of certain men that "came down from Judea and taught the brethren, 'Unless you are circumcised according to the custom of Moses, you cannot be saved.'"

DO OR DIE!

Some of the disciples were sent to Jerusalem to address the issue. After much discussion, Peter stood and said:

> Men and brethren, you know that a good while ago God chose among us, that by my mouth the Gentiles should hear the word of the gospel and believe. So God, who knows the heart, acknowledged them [the Gentiles] by giving them the Holy Spirit, just as He did to us, and made no distinction between us and them, purifying their hearts by faith.
>
> —ACTS 15:7–9

The law required circumcision, but all the new covenant demanded was faith. Remember, the law and works have always been the opposite of grace and mercy.

- The law says, "Follow the rules." Grace says, "It is a free gift."

- The law says, "See your sin and shame." Grace says, "God accepts you as you are."

- The law brings the consciousness of sin. Grace brings the awareness of righteousness.

- The law says, "Do or die." Grace says, "Accept Jesus as Savior and live."

THE VINE AND THE BRANCHES

It is not our strength that produces life but His.

Just before the crucifixion, Jesus had a meal with His disciples and gave them one of the greatest lessons found in the Gospels. He told them that they were not the vine and they were not the fruit—they were the branches.

We are an outlet for God's power, not the power itself. Jesus said:

> I am the true vine, and My Father is the vinedresser. Every branch in Me that does not bear fruit He takes away; and every branch that bears fruit He prunes, that it may bear more fruit. You are already clean because of the word which I have spoken to you. Abide in Me, and I in you. As the branch cannot bear fruit of itself, unless it abides in the vine, neither can you, unless you abide in Me. I am the vine, you are the branches. He who abides in Me, and I in him, bears much fruit; for without Me you can do nothing.
>
> —JOHN 15:1–5

God's purpose as the "vinedresser" is to keep the vine clean. The pruning of sin is the result not of our effort but of His. All we are required to do is surrender.

Some Christians are struggling to bear fruit, but no branch has the power to make that happen. Jesus was saying, "You don't bear the fruit. I do. But I give you the privilege of holding it. The fruit is Mine. The vine is Mine. The branch is simply hooked onto Me. That's all."

Someone once asked, "If God is doing all the work, then what is my job?"

"Hang on!" I replied.

The vine supplies life to the branches, and the branch has the privilege of holding the fruit. In effect, our job is to become "fruit hangers."

Take a close look at what is attached to the branch. It is the fruit of the Holy Spirit—not of the flesh. We become the channel through which love, joy, peace, and other spiritual fruit are given to the world (Gal. 5:22–23).

What is the result of our branch-vine relationship? When we understand it and make the Lord the source of our lives, He answers our prayers. Jesus said:

> If you abide in Me, and My words abide in you, you will ask what you desire, and it shall be done for you.
>
> —JOHN 15:7

Never forget that Jesus said, "Without Me you can do nothing" (John 15:5). That is true before, during, and after salvation.

The vine is strong and the branch is weak, but branches are what God uses to deliver His fruit to the world. In the words of the apostle Paul:

> God has chosen the foolish things of the world to put to shame the wise, and God has chosen the weak things of the world to put to shame the things which are mighty; and the base things of the world and the things which are despised God has chosen, and the things which are not, to bring to nothing the things that are, that no flesh should glory in His presence.
>
> —1 CORINTHIANS 1:27–29

"Free Indeed"

Without the blood of Christ and God's grace it would be impossible for us to have victory over sin. Paul explained what it is like to fight sin in the flesh. "For we know that the law is spiritual, but I am carnal, sold under sin" (Rom. 7:14). He added, "For I know that in me (that is, in my flesh) nothing good dwells; for to will is present with me, but how to perform what is good I do not find" (Rom. 7:18).

Our flesh contains nothing that is good, and our righteousness is as filthy rags (Isa. 64:6). We can't make ourselves good enough to please God.

I remember praying, "Lord, there must be something I can do to please You."

"My greatest pleasure is when you allow Me to do the work," He said.

I once heard a story about a Russian pastor who was thrown in prison by communist officials for preaching the gospel in the former Soviet Union. They did not allow this great saint of God to see another human being, and they fed him by pushing the food under the door. Years and years passed, and one day the Lord appeared to this man in prison.

The man was so grateful to the Lord for coming to see him. He asked Him, "Is there anything I can give You to say thank You?"

"No, everything is Mine," the Lord responded. "There is nothing you can give Me."

"But, Lord, there must be something I can give You to say thank You."

"There is nothing you can give Me," the Lord repeated. "Your very body belongs to Me. Your very life is Mine."

But the man asked again, "Oh, please, there must be one thing I can give You."

Then the Lord said, "There is. Give Me your sins. That's all I want."

That's all He wants—our surrender. We turn our sins over to Him because He is the only One who can subdue them. The Bible says:

> Who is a God like You, pardoning iniquity and passing over the transgression of the remnant of His heritage? He does not retain His anger forever, because He delights in mercy. He will again have compassion on us, and will subdue our iniquities.
> —MICAH 7:18–19

Paul's solution to his struggle with sin was to turn it over to Christ. He said, "For the law of the Spirit of life in Christ Jesus has made me free from the law of sin and death. For what the law could not do in that it was weak through the flesh, God did by sending His own Son in the likeness of sinful flesh, on account of sin: He condemned sin in the flesh, that the righteous requirement of the law might be fulfilled in us who do not walk according to the flesh but according to the Spirit" (Rom. 8:2–4).

Some people say, "I've tried to pray, and I have failed. I've tried to read the Word, and my mind wanders. I've tried to get rid of my habits, and I can't."

Again and again they say, "Lord, I'll try one more time." And they continue to fail.

After many years they finally pray the only prayer God wants to hear: "Lord, I can't do it. You will have to do the work." And they finally learn what Philippians 2:13 really means:

> It is God who works in you both to will and to do for His good pleasure.

Suddenly they are transformed and find how easy it is to live for Jesus. Jesus said, "My yoke is easy and My burden is light" (Matt. 11:30). He also said:

Whoever commits sin is a slave of sin. And a slave does not abide in the house forever, but a son abides forever. Therefore if the Son makes you free, you shall be free indeed.

—John 8:34–36

Saint, remember that you will never be able to solve your own problems. The Scriptures say it is "not by might nor by power, but by My Spirit" (Zech. 4:6).

A Covenant to Keep

1. What are the areas in your life in which you find it difficult to trust God? If you are struggling in any of the areas listed below, describe the reason it is hard to trust God in that area. Circle the areas where you need to surrender and trust the blood of Jesus to bring healing to that situation.

   My marriage:

   _____

   _____

   My family:

   _____

   _____

   My work:

   _____

   _____

   My health:

   _____

   _____

   My spiritual life:

   _____

   _____

My parents:

_____

_____

Other:

_____

_____

Because of God's great mercy and love for us, "even when we were dead in trespasses, [He] made us alive together with Christ... and raised us up together, and made us sit together in the heavenly places in Christ Jesus" (Eph. 2:5–6).

Heaven will be ours not because of what we have done but because of "the exceeding riches of His grace in His kindness toward us in Christ Jesus" (Eph. 2:7). The blood of Christ covers our sin, and we receive forgiveness through faith because of the grace of God. It is a message that every believer needs to understand. We had nothing to do with earning our salvation. Religion says "Do." Jesus says "Done!"

2. What kind of image did you have of God as you grew up?

- A God to fear

- An angry and punishing God

- A loving and forgiving Father

- A distant and remote God

- A powerful God

Though God occasionally chastises us for our good, He is always gentle, kind, and loving to His children. Read Psalm 103:6–13. Describe all the Father's qualities that this psalm mentions.

_____

_____

3. All the Lord wants is our surrender. We turn our sins over to Him because He is the only One who can subdue them. The Bible says, "Who is a God like You, pardoning iniquity and passing over the transgression of the remnant of His heritage? He does not retain His anger forever, because He delights in mercy. He will again have compassion on us, and will subdue our iniquities" (Mic. 7:18–19).

God delights in showing mercy. In your own words, describe the experience of mercy you received from the Lord, who pardoned your transgressions.

_____

_____

Thank You, Jesus, for the freedom and rest I have found in You. I surrender my will afresh and anew to You today. Holy Spirit, continue showing me what it means to rest in Your presence. Amen.

Chapter 15

THERE'S STRENGTH
in the BLOOD

A MOVING STORY IS told about the events of a typical Sunday
evening service in a local church. The pastor had invited a
childhood friend, who was also a minister, to be the guest
speaker that evening. After a few of the usual Sunday evening
hymns, the church's pastor slowly stood to his feet, walked over to
the pulpit, and briefly introduced the guest minister. He welcomed
his lifelong friend to the pulpit and quickly returned to his seat.

With that, an elderly man stepped up to the pulpit and began to
speak. "A father, his son, and a friend of his son were sailing off the
Pacific coast," he began, "when a fast-approaching storm blocked
any attempt to get back to shore. The waves were so high that, even
though the father was an experienced sailor, he could not keep the
boat upright. Suddenly both boys were swept out into the ocean."

The old man hesitated for a moment before continuing. As he
paused, he made eye contact with two teenagers who appeared
interested for the first time since the service began.

"Grabbing a rescue line," he continued, "the father had to make
the most excruciating decision of his life: to which boy would he
throw the other end of the line? He only had seconds to make the
decision. The father knew that his son was a Christian, and he also
knew that his son's friend was not. The agony of the decision before
him tore at his heart as the perilous waves surged around him.

"Suddenly, the father yelled out, 'I love you, son!' as he threw the
lifeline to his son's friend. Struggling against the raging seas, he
pulled the line in inch by inch. By the time he finally pulled the
friend of his son back to the boat, his son had disappeared beyond

155

the stormy swells into the black of night. His body was never recovered."

By this time, the two teenagers were even more attentive and sitting straighter in the pew, waiting for the next words to come out of the old man's mouth.

Resuming the story, the old man said, "In that moment of decision the father knew his son would step into eternity with Jesus, and he could not bear the thought of his son's friend stepping into an eternity without Jesus. Therefore, he sacrificed his son. How great is the love of God that He should do the same for us."

With that, the old man closed his Bible, turned around, and sat back down in his chair as a cloud of silence filled the room. Within minutes after the service ended, the two teenagers were at the old man's side.

"That was a nice story, sir," one of the boys said politely, "but I don't think it was very realistic for a father to give up his son's life in hopes that the other boy would become a Christian."

"Well, you've got a point there," the old man replied, glancing down at his worn Bible. A big smile broadened on his narrow face as he once again looked up at the boys and said, "It sure isn't very realistic, is it? But I'm standing here today to tell you that this story gives me a glimpse of what it must have been like for God to give up His Son for me. You see, I was the one to whom the rope was thrown. I was the son's friend."

This story depicts the sacrificial act of a father for the good of one who was eternally lost. Scripture records that our loving heavenly Father made an even greater sacrifice when He gave His only begotten Son as the supreme sacrifice.

> He who did not spare His own Son, but delivered Him up for us all, how shall He not with Him also freely give us all things?
>
> —ROMANS 8:32

> But God commendeth his love toward us, in that, while we
> were yet sinners, Christ died for us.
>
> —ROMANS 5:8, KJV

My oldest daughter, Jessica, is now a beautiful grown woman,
but when she was just a toddler, I remember taking her for a walk
in the woods.

As we were about to walk up a little hill, I reached down and
took hold of her hand. I didn't want her to slip and fall.

Jessica's little hand was too weak to hold on to mine. She was
depending on my strength to help her reach the top of the hill.

Then the Holy Spirit whispered to my heart, "Who is holding
your hand?"

As I thought about it, I said, "You are, Lord."

How true it is. All of us are like my Jessica. We're too weak to
hold on to His hand. He holds on to our hands.

The Bible says, "For I, the LORD your God, will hold your right
hand, saying to you, 'Fear not, I will help you'" (Isa. 41:13).

The Old Covenant promised it, and so did the New. Jesus said,
"And I give them eternal life, and they shall never perish; neither
shall anyone snatch them out of My hand" (John 10:28).

The first time I read that Scripture passage I said, "Thank You,
Lord, for reaching down and holding me."

Several years later, I was studying the passage again, and I began
to praise the Lord as I noticed what the next verse said:

> My Father, who has given them to Me, is greater than all; and
> no one is able to snatch them out of My Father's hand.
>
> —JOHN 10:29

Not only is Jesus holding my hand, but the Father is holding it
too. When He reaches out to you, you can be sure that He will
never let go. The only time Jesus will let you go is when you push
Him away.

Not only does the Lord hold us, but He will also lead us on the right path. You are God's possession, and He will protect you and sustain you. The psalmist tells us:

> The steps of a good man are ordered by the Lord, and He delights in his way. Though he fall, he shall not be utterly cast down; for the Lord upholds him with His hand.
>
> —Psalm 37:23–24

> For You have delivered my soul from death. Have You not kept my feet from falling, that I may walk before God in the light of the living?
>
> —Psalm 56:13

God's grace is not something that happens in a moment of time and then disappears. It is part of our process of growing. Peter said that we are to "grow in the grace and knowledge of our Lord and Savior Jesus Christ" (2 Pet. 3:18).

How is it possible to grow in grace? By understanding God's love, His patience, His mercy, and His acceptance for us. In hundreds of ways the Lord says, "I won't give up on you. I love you, and I forgive you."

When we fail, He reaches down again and takes us in His arms. That is how we continue to grow in grace.

Grace and Truth

The Word says that Christ was filled with grace and truth.

> And the Word became flesh and dwelt among us, and we beheld His glory, the glory as of the only begotten of the Father, full of grace and truth.
>
> —John 1:14

Christ revealed that grace and truth to us through His completed work on the cross.

For the law was given through Moses, but grace and truth
came through Jesus Christ.

—JOHN 1:17

When the Lord was teaching a group of people in the temple
courts of Jerusalem, the Pharisees brought to Him a woman who
had been caught in adultery, and they said, "Now Moses, in the law,
commanded us that such should be stoned. But what do You say?"
(John 8:5).

Jesus ignored their question and bent over to write something on
the ground with His finger. When they continued questioning Him,
He stood up and said, "He who is without sin among you, let him
throw a stone at her first" (John 8:7).

As He continued to write on the ground, the critics began to
walk away until only Jesus and the woman were left. He turned to
her and asked:

> "Woman, where are those accusers of yours? Has no one con-
> demned you?" She said, "No one, Lord." And Jesus said to her,
> "Neither do I condemn you; go and sin no more."
>
> —JOHN 8:10–11

He said, "Neither do I condemn you"—that's grace.
"Go and sin no more"—that's truth.

She saw His grace and decided to sin no more. When we truly
see His love and grace, we will also want to follow Him and forsake
our sin.

The Lord never tells us to "sin no more"—or do any other thing—
unless He knows we can do it. And because He gives us the power
to obey His commands, He knows we can do it. This way, every
command is really a promise.

FEAR AND TREMBLING

Nearly every time I discuss the grace of God someone will ask, "Doesn't the Bible tell us that we have to work out our own salvation?"

Here is what Paul said: "Work out your own salvation with fear and trembling" (Phil. 2:12). But we need to look at the context of that statement.

> Therefore, my beloved, as you have always obeyed, not as in my presence only, but now much more in my absence, work out your own salvation with fear and trembling.
>
> —PHILIPPIANS 2:12

But that is not the end of the story. It is not our work but the Lord's that makes it possible. The next verse says, "For it is God who works in you both to will and to do for His good pleasure" (Phil. 2:13).

So the Christian life is really working out or exercising the salvation that God has provided because of Christ's blood—and He gives us both the desire and strength to do what pleases Him.

Here is the amazing thing: when we let God do the work in us, then He enables us to work out His salvation.

> For we are His workmanship, created in Christ Jesus for good works, which God prepared beforehand that we should walk in them.
>
> —EPHESIANS 2:10

The Lord is not against our efforts, but they must be a product of His workmanship—His grace. In fact, one of the Lord's purposes for your salvation is to have you live a "blameless" life.

> He chose us in Him before the foundation of the world, that we should be holy and without blame before Him.
>
> —EPHESIANS 1:4

Good works will be a by-product in the lives of those who know God's unmerited favor. And the Lord gives us the will to love Him, obey Him, and serve Him. We can't follow the Lord without Him first touching us. Jesus said, "No one can come to Me unless the Father who sent Me draws him" (John 6:44).

We can't love Him without the Holy Spirit giving us the love with which to love Him.

> Now hope does not disappoint, because the love of God has been poured out in our hearts by the Holy Spirit who was given to us.
>
> —ROMANS 5:5

When you experience God's love, love will flow out of you to those around you. When you find His acceptance, you will accept others. When you experience giving, you will give.

It all comes down to one simple thing: God works it in, and we work it out.

We let Him pour in that we may pour out. First we cooperate; then we respond. But the Bible makes it clear that we can't work to earn our salvation.

> Now to him who works, the wages are not counted as grace but as debt. But to him who does not work but believes on Him who justifies the ungodly, his faith is accounted for righteousness.
>
> —ROMANS 4:4–5

The Lord does not owe us something because we do good works. He will never be indebted to anyone. We don't say, "I did it, Lord. Here's my bill." If we work for something, it is not grace.

There is nothing in us that even desires God without His first putting the desire within us (John 6:44). God won't honor a person who says, "I'm going to pray, and I'm going to make it." God says,

"That is the flesh, and I don't want it." God won't accept works or prayers that come from the flesh.

Total Dependence

One day as I was reading Psalm 119, I noticed the way David was saying, "I cannot do it, Lord. Only You can." I began to see in this psalm his total dependence on God, which I have emphasized below.

- "*Deal bountifully* with Your servant, that I may live and keep Your word" (v. 17).

- "*Open my eyes*, that I may see wondrous things from Your law" (v. 18).

- "I am a stranger in the earth; *do not hide* Your commandments from me" (v. 19).

- "*Remove from me* reproach and contempt, for I have kept Your testimonies" (v. 22).

- "My soul clings to the dust; *revive me* according to Your word" (v. 25).

- "*Make me understand* the way of Your precepts; so shall I meditate on Your wonderful works" (v. 27).

- "*Remove from me* the way of lying, and *grant me* Your law graciously" (v. 29).

- "I will run the course of Your commandments, *for You shall* enlarge my heart" (v. 32).

- "*Teach me*, O Lord, the way of Your statutes, and I shall keep it to the end" (v. 33).

- "*Give me understanding,* and I shall keep Your law; indeed, I shall observe it with my whole heart" (v. 34).

- *"Make me walk* in the path of Your commandments, for I delight in it" (v. 35).

- *"Incline my heart* to Your testimonies, and not to covetousness" (v. 36).

- *"Turn away my eyes* from looking at worthless things, and revive me in Your way" (v. 37).

- *"Establish Your word* to Your servant, who is devoted to fearing You" (v. 38).

- *"Turn away my reproach* which I dread, for Your judgments are good" (v. 39).

- "Behold, I long for Your precepts; *revive me in Your righteousness*" (v. 40).

- *"Let my heart be blameless* regarding Your statutes, that I may not be ashamed" (v. 80).

- *"Hold me up*, and I shall be safe, and I shall observe Your statutes continually" (v. 117).

- "Be surety for Your servant for good; *do not let* the proud oppress me" (v. 122).

- "Direct my steps by Your word, and *let no iniquity have dominion over me*" (v. 133).

Who is doing the work? David or the Lord?

We see clearly here that David is saying, "Only the Lord can." All we have to do is surrender and let Him do it. So like David, ask the Lord today to come and work His grace in you, and say, "Lord, direct my steps so that I can walk with You." (See Psalm 119:133.)

True prayer is impossible without the Holy Spirit's help. Like so many Christians, I thought I could seek the Lord on my own until one day I read Psalm 119:176, which states:

> I have gone astray like a lost sheep; seek Your servant, for I do not forget Your commandments.

When it comes to seeking the Lord, remember that He seeks us first. As A. W. Tozer said, "Before a man can seek God, God must first have sought the man."[1]

From that day until now I pray daily, "Lord Jesus, touch me so that I can call on You. Give me the strength to seek You today."

David himself said in the Book of Psalms, "Quicken us, and we will call upon thy name" (Ps. 80:18, KJV). It is not your doing. It is His grace.

I heard an amazing definition of grace one night on a Christian television program. What I learned is the subject of my next chapter.

A COVENANT TO KEEP

1. The Bible says, "For I, the LORD your God, will hold your right hand, saying to you, 'Fear not, I will help you'" (Isa. 41:13). The Old Covenant promised it, and so did the New Covenant. Jesus said, "And I give them eternal life, and they shall never perish; neither shall anyone snatch them out of My hand. My Father, who has given them to Me, is greater than all; and no one is able to snatch them out of My Father's hand" (John 10:28–29).

   What are some areas of your life (or people in your life) that you need to place in your Father's hands? List them on the lines below.

   _____

   _____

2. Just as David declared his total dependence on God in Psalm 119, so we should also declare our dependence on God for everything in our lives. Find a psalm that best describes your heart's cry for depending upon the Father. On the lines below, write down the reference and then write the attributes that best describe your feelings of dependency on God.

   _____

   _____

3. The Master's touch is so important in our lives. His hand delivers us from every bondage in life. Remember, His shed blood flowed through His hands for us. Many scriptures talk about God's hands and His touch. Read

Psalm 37:23–24; Isaiah 41:13; and John 10:29. Then describe what a touch from God means to you.

To me, His touch means…

_____

_____

Heavenly Father, like David, I declare my total dependence on You. I can do nothing apart from Your Holy Spirit. Remove from me contempt, lying, malice, self-reliance, and any other negative character traits that separate me from You. Holy Spirit, lead me and guide me in all I say and do. May the words that come out of my mouth and my actions reflect the Son. In Jesus' precious name, amen.

Chapter 16

FIVE AREAS in LIFE to APPLY the BLOOD of CHRIST

W'VE COVERED A lot of ground regarding the blood of Jesus—not only *why* a blood covenant was required but also that there is protection, salvation, cleansing, power, new life, freedom, rest, and strength in the blood. Now I want to teach you the five areas of your life to which you can apply the blood. Once you get this teaching down in your spirit, it will change your life.

The Scriptures say very clearly that we as believers have the authority to apply the blood to five areas of our lives:

1. The blood covers *you.*

2. The blood covers *your house*, meaning your family.

3. The blood covers *your possessions.*

4. The blood covers *your endeavors*, meaning the work of your hands and everything you touch.

5. The blood covers *your influence*, meaning your increase.

Remember that Job offered blood sacrifices for each of his children by name, lest they had cursed God in their hearts (Job 1:5). As we read further in verses 6–10, we see an amazing scene take place: "a day when the sons of God came to present themselves before the LORD, and Satan came also among them" (v. 6, KJV).

Now, when the enemy came in before God, and the Lord asked, "Have you considered My servant Job?" Satan said, "I cannot even touch him because You built a hedge around him."

Do you remember how the hedge was built? The hedge of protection was built when Job applied the blood. So when we apply the blood, the Lord builds a hedge around us.

Satan said, "I cannot touch him, I cannot touch his household, and I cannot touch his possessions because You've placed a hedge about him and all that he has on every side. You have blessed the work of his hands, and his substance is increased in the land." (See Job 1:10.) This shows there are five areas the devil recognizes that he cannot touch. If the blood is applied, he cannot get through that hedge of protection.

When you apply the blood, demons cannot touch you! Satan said, "Not only have You blessed his person, his family, and his possessions, but You've also blessed the work of his hands (meaning his job and bank account)."

God said He will rebuke the devourer for your sake. Satan will not touch the fruit of your ground—your money. There will be no holes in your pockets.

The enemy said, "You've also put a hedge about him so that his substance is increased in the land," meaning Job had a lot of influence and a lot of friends.

APPLY THE BLOOD DAILY

As a quick review, we see the blood introduced in Genesis 3:21 when God covers Adam and Eve with animal skins, introducing redemption, protection, and restoration. Then the Bible says Cain came and offered God a gift of fruit and vegetables, and it was rejected; but Abel offered God blood, the firstfruits of his flock, and God accepted his sacrifice. Abel knew from his father by faith that God accepts blood because He is the covenant-making, covenant-keeping God—and you can't have a covenant without the blood.

Then in Genesis 7 we read about Noah going into the ark with seven each of every clean animal and two of every unclean animal: seven for sacrifice, two for preservation. In Genesis 8:20 we read that when Noah came out of the ark, he built an altar and offered blood, and the curse was broken. He then entered into blood covenant with God.

When Abraham went into the Promised Land, the first thing he did was build an altar and offer an animal and blood, knowing that God would not keep His promise to him without the blood. (See Genesis 12.) Then, when Isaac entered the Promised Land, God appeared and made a covenant with him, saying, "Now, what I've given your father I give to you." (See Genesis 26:2–5.) Isaac built an altar, and so again the blood was offered and the promises were guaranteed. How? By covenant.

When Jacob went into the Promised Land after he returned from Laban's house, the first thing he did was build an altar (Gen. 33:18–20). Why? To guarantee the promises of God.

These patriarchs recognized that you can have no approach, no favor with God, without the blood. God will not hear your prayer without the blood.

What the patriarchs experienced their descendants also experienced when they were coming out of Egypt in Exodus 12. God told the Israelites to apply the blood of a lamb to the doorposts and lintels of their homes, and when He saw the blood, He would pass over them and spare them the judgment He would execute on Egypt. God said, "I will not allow Satan to destroy you when I see the blood" (v. 23, my paraphrase).

In Exodus 24:8, God commanded Moses to apply blood on all Israel—three million people—and His covenant with Israel was sealed. Then, beginning in Exodus chapter 25, God gave Moses instructions to build a tabernacle for Him to dwell in. In other words, once the blood was applied, God began to dwell among His people.

Before the covenant was sealed, Moses had to go up the

mountain by himself. God said, "Don't bring anybody with you. Nobody is allowed to be near Me except you." If anyone—or anything, including animals—even approached the mountain, they were killed. After the covenant was sealed, because of the blood, God told Moses, "Don't come up anymore; I'm coming down."

God now dwells among His people because of the blood. That means when you apply the blood to your home, God will dwell in that home. God's presence will be in your home.

The first thing John the Baptist says in John 1:29 is, "Behold! The Lamb of God." The same blood covenant in the Old Covenant that went on for hundreds of years in the tabernacle and the temple, Jesus perfected in the New Covenant when He declared Himself to be the sacrifice and died on the cross of Calvary.

In John 6, Jesus said He came for one purpose: to die on the cross. Then He said, "For my flesh is meat indeed, and my blood is drink indeed" (v. 55, KJV).

REDEMPTION IS THE DOORWAY

In his first epistle, Peter declares something about the mystery of redemption—this marvelous gift we receive when we are born again through the shed blood of Jesus:

> Knowing that you were not *redeemed* with corruptible things, like silver or gold, from your aimless conduct received by tradition from your fathers, but with the precious blood of Christ, as of a lamb without blemish and without spot.
> —1 PETER 1:18–19, EMPHASIS ADDED

Now, as believers, we cannot rest until we understand the full knowledge of redemption. Once you are redeemed, then you're reconciled. Once you are reconciled, then you're cleansed. Once you are cleansed, then you're sanctified. Once you are sanctified, then you experience victory. And when you are victorious in Christ, you will experience *life* more abundantly—all because of the blood.

Redemption is the door that leads to all the others. Redemption means you now belong to God; you were paid for by His blood. From the top of your head to the soles of your feet, your body is the temple of the Holy Ghost, not the temple of devils.

You Are God's Property

If you have been redeemed, you are now God's property. Jesus is your Lord, Master, and Owner. Your body is no longer your own; it's His temple, purchased by the blood of the Lamb. Jesus owns the very hairs on your head—that is why He counts them.

The people who are demon-oppressed are those who don't know what redemption means in their lives. You need to tell the devil where he stands. Tell him, "I don't belong to you or to myself; I belong to Jesus now. Complete authority is His!"

The Bible doesn't say my enemies are chasing me; it says I'm chasing them. David said, "I'm pursuing my enemies," not the other way around. We are more than conquerors in Christ Jesus! The righteous are as bold as lions.

Don't you dare be afraid of the devil; he's afraid of you! God said He would soon crush Satan under your feet (Rom. 16:20). The enemy has nothing on you. He's a defeated foe, and he knows it. It's time for you to realize it and tell him off. You are redeemed. You are royalty—a royal priesthood, a holy nation (1 Pet. 2:9). Don't you dare lower yourself! You are a child of the King of kings and Lord of lords!

What Did the Blood Accomplish?

The blood of Jesus accomplished many miraculous things for us as believers.

1. The blood opened Jesus' grave. Hebrews 13:20 speaks of "the God of peace who brought up our Lord Jesus from the dead, that great Shepherd of the sheep, through the blood of the everlasting covenant." Jesus' blood opened His own grave.

2. The blood opened heaven. Hebrews 9:12 tells us, "With His own blood He entered the Most Holy Place once for all, having obtained eternal redemption." Jesus entered heaven with His blood. Prior to that, heaven was closed. For thousands of years the saints of the Old Testament could not enter heaven; they had to go to Paradise and wait. The only ones who went to heaven by the sovereignty of God were Enoch and Elijah. But Jesus opened heaven when He carried His blood. And so today by the power of the blood, when we die as believers, we enter heaven.

In the old covenant the angels had to fight the principalities of the air before they could bring answers to prayer. Today we don't need battles to receive answers because the way has been opened by the blood.

3. The blood opened our hearts. That same blood not only opened the grave of Christ (Heb. 13:20) and opened heaven (Heb. 9:12), but it also has the power to open your heart. Did you know it's harder to open the hearts of men than to open the grave? But now, God has the power to open the hearts of men by the blood of Jesus.

The apostle Peter powerfully tells us that it is the blood that opened our hearts to salvation.

> Knowing that you were not redeemed with corruptible things, like silver or gold, from your aimless conduct received by tradition from your fathers, but with the precious blood of Christ, as of a lamb without blemish and without spot.
> —1 Peter 1:18–19

4. The blood of Jesus satisfied the Law and the righteousness of God. Romans 3:25–26 (NIV) tells us, "God presented Christ as a sacrifice of atonement, through the shedding of his blood—to be received by faith. He did this to demonstrate his righteousness, because in his forbearance he had left the sins committed beforehand unpunished—he did it to demonstrate his righteousness at the present time, so as to be just and the one who justifies those who have faith in Jesus."

5. Jesus overcame the power of sin by the blood. In Hebrews 9:22 (NIV) we read, "In fact, the law requires that nearly everything be cleansed with blood, and without the shedding of blood there is no forgiveness."

6. Jesus defeated death by the blood. First Corinthians 15:54–55 says, "So when this corruptible has put on incorruption, and this mortal has put on immortality, then shall be brought to pass the saying that is written: 'Death is swallowed up in victory.' 'O Death, where is your sting? O Hades, where is your victory?'"

7. Jesus destroyed the power of Satan by the power of His blood. Hebrews 2:14–15 states, "Inasmuch then as the children have partaken of flesh and blood, He Himself likewise shared in the same, that through death He might destroy him who had the power of death, that is, the devil, and release those who through fear of death were all their lifetime subject to bondage."

8. The power of death and hell came to an end through the blood. Revelation 20:14 tells us, "Then Death and Hades were cast into the lake of fire." And, once again, 1 Corinthians 15:54–55 says, "Death is swallowed up in victory. O Death, where is your sting? O Hades, where is your victory?"

9. Because of the blood, we can approach the throne of grace. Finally, beloved, we can now approach the Judge of all—Jesus the Mediator—through the sprinkled blood, as we read in Hebrews 12:22–24:

> But you have come to Mount Zion and to the city of the living God, the heavenly Jerusalem, to an innumerable company of angels, to the general assembly and church of the firstborn who are registered in heaven, to God the Judge of all, to the spirits of just men made perfect, to Jesus the Mediator of the new covenant, and to the blood of sprinkling that speaks better things than that of Abel.

So, we not only come to the general assembly of the firstborn and so forth, but we also come to the Judge of all, to Jesus our Mediator, and to the blood—through "a new and living way" (Heb. 10:19–20).

AN AMAZING DECLARATION

Only the blood of Jesus can liberate the human heart. We were enslaved under the hostility of Satan's power, enslaved under the curse of the law and sin. Now we are redeemed through the blood. When you make this amazing declaration—when you *say* your redemption ("Let the redeemed of the LORD say so" [Ps. 107:2])—this declaration is heard and begins its work of deliverance. This declaration brings the soul out of prison. It brings liberty to the believer. When you speak your redemption, you defeat the powers of hell.

The devil cannot hear your thoughts, but he can hear your words. Say out loud, "Devil, you cannot touch me. I am redeemed!" Have you ever noticed that the Scripture says *say so*, not *think so*? The blood that prevailed so mightily over hell, so mightily in heaven, is all-powerful and can change your life.

Listen to how the apostle Paul put it:

> Being justified freely by his grace through the redemption that is in Christ Jesus: Whom God hath set forth to be a propitiation through faith in his blood, to declare his righteousness for the remission of sins that are past, through the forbearance of God.
>
> —ROMANS 3:24–25, KJV

This is the work of reconciliation. And what is reconciliation? It is the removal and destruction of sin. Reconciliation renders sin powerless. If you don't have the revealed truth in your life that you are redeemed, you will keep going back to the same old stuff, and the same old sins will still have you by the throat. But the second you claim your redemption—the second you take your possession—reconciliation sets in.

The minute reconciliation sets in, sin loses its hold. When you come into reconciliation, you then walk into holiness and victory. You experience the love of God because His love begins to bestow favor. Oh, precious ones, I'm talking about how God sees you through the blood. You have to believe it! You have to live it! You have to live in a state of repentance! Sin is powerless when you know your redemption—when you read the Scriptures and really understand who you are.

In the next chapter we will look at how Christians can keep themselves free from demonic oppression. Here's the sobering truth: even though we are redeemed, our actions can open the door to the devil.

A COVENANT TO KEEP

1. Listed below are some of the benefits available to believers through the shed blood of Jesus. Look up each Scripture reference and draw a line from that reference to the benefit listed in that verse.

John 6:54	Peace
1 Corinthians 1:18	Access
Galatians 3:13–14	Eternal life
Ephesians 2:16	The power of God
Ephesians 2:18	Ability to overcome the enemy
Colossians 1:20	The promise of the Spirit
Hebrews 10:19	Reconciliation
Revelation 12:11	Boldness to enter the Holiest

2. Now it's time to thank the Lord for all He has made available to us through His blood. Either use your own words or pray the prayer listed here:

Dear Lord, thank You for all You have given us through Your precious blood. Because You laid down Your life, we can have victory over sin and the devil here on earth and eternal life with You in heaven forever. In the name of Jesus we pray. Amen.

Chapter 17

FREEDOM FROM
DEMONIC OPPRESSION

VERYWHERE I GO to minister, I hear the questions, "Can a Christian be oppressed by a demon spirit?" and "Can a Christian have a devil?" The answer to both is yes—to be specific, not in their spirits, but Christians can be oppressed in their soulish realms if they open a door. Demons cannot come in if the door is shut.

When the Lord entered into your heart, your spirit was saved. And the Bible says that "he who is joined to the Lord is one spirit with Him" (1 Cor. 6:17), meaning that your spirit man cannot be oppressed or possessed by a demon. I want you to understand the distinction: The soul *is being* saved. The body *will be* saved. But the spirit *was* saved. That means my soul is being saved continually. So, we're dealing with something very important in this chapter.

KEEP WATCH OVER YOUR SOUL

Second Peter 2:18–19 (NIV) explains why people are oppressed:

> For they mouth empty, boastful words and, by appealing to the lustful desires of the flesh, they entice people who are just escaping from those who live in error. They promise them freedom, while they themselves are slaves of depravity—for "people are slaves to whatever has mastered them."

In short, people are oppressed because in some way they have opened a door to the demonic. Here Peter is talking about false teachers that speak "empty, boastful words" and promise people freedom while they themselves are slaves of depravity. But the second portion of this verse also says something very important: "People are slaves to whatever has mastered them" (v. 19, NIV).

I have lived in this blessed faith called the Christian life for more than half a century now, and I've learned that if we allow ourselves to become entangled in the things of this world, we get in trouble. We must live a daily life with Jesus and daily be renewed in the Spirit.

We know that the spirit of the believer is already one with the Lord, and the body the Lord will take care of on resurrection morning. But it's the soul you have to worry about. What is the soul? The soul is what I *think*, what I *feel*, and what I *want*.

Every day, each of us makes a decision: Am I going to submit to the Spirit of God in my spirit, or will I submit to my body, which is connected to the world? If my spirit man is connected to the Holy Spirit, one with the Holy Spirit, all is well. My body is the part of me that is connected to the world. And every day my soul decides, Which side will I join today?

It's quite simple, isn't it? That is why Scripture says "people are slaves to whatever has mastered them" (2 Pet. 2:19, NIV). The New King James translation puts it this way: "for by whom a person is overcome, by him also he is brought into bondage." And that's also why Ephesians 4:27 says, "[Do not] give place to the devil," because it is possible to give the devil a place.

First Peter 5:8–9 says something very important:

> Be sober, be vigilant; because your adversary the devil walks about like a roaring lion, seeking whom he may devour. Resist him, steadfast in the faith, knowing that the same sufferings are experienced by your brotherhood in the world.

To "be sober" means to be well balanced, to be vigilant or cautious because our enemy the devil is walking around like a lion looking for someone to devour. The Word says we resist him by being steadfast in the faith.

In Matthew 12:43–45 the Lord talks about how demons go looking for vacancy. What are they looking for? You have to understand that demons are very territorial. When we got saved, they left—but they don't give up easily. They come back and say, "You know what? I'm going to go back and visit my old house to see if it's vacant."

What are they looking for? The Word—not signs or wonders and not the gifts, because a lot of people who have the gifts are still bound. The Word of God is what keeps us free. It is what keeps us strong in the Lord. The Bible is clear that those who love the Word will never be in bondage.

> Great peace have they which love thy law: and nothing shall offend them.
>
> —Psalm 119:165, kjv

As freewill agents, people do things that lead them into bondage. It doesn't matter whether or not these actions are intentional; certain activities and behaviors open the door to demonic oppression. Now, again, as a Christian you cannot be possessed or oppressed in your spirit. However, you most definitely can be oppressed in your soul realm and in your physical body. But what opens the door?

Things That Open the Door to Oppression

Rebellion. This is a very serious sin that always brings demonic torment. We see this in the life of King Saul. He was bitterly jealous of David, who was anointed to be king in his place, and in 1 Samuel 16:14 we read, "But the Spirit of the Lord departed from Saul, and an evil spirit *from the Lord* troubled him" (kjv, emphasis added).

Abnormal sexual activity. According to the Bible, any sexual activity outside of marriage is off-limits and therefore abnormal. Hebrews 13:4 and Galatians 5:19–21 make it plain that fornicators, adulterers, and those who practice "uncleanness" and lewd behavior will face God's judgment, which means they are open to being tormented by the devil.

Occult activity. When people read horoscopes, use Ouija boards, receive tarot card readings and palm readings, watch demonic programs or movies, listen to demonic music, and engage in other such activities, it can bring destruction and disaster into their lives. I remember a girl back in Canada who would watch things like *Frankenstein* and other horror movies every Friday night. Naturally, the devil came, and the girl was oppressed by demons. She came to one of my meetings, and I had to get the devil out of her. Occult activity is very dangerous.

Abuse of the tongue. When people talk about things they shouldn't, it opens the door to the demonic realm. Proverbs 12:13 (KJV) says, "The wicked is snared by the transgression of his lips." Proverbs 13:3 says, "He who guards his mouth preserves his life, but he who opens wide his lips shall have destruction." So be careful what you say because it can open the door to demons.

Fear. In 1 John 4:18 we read, "There is no fear in love; but perfect love casts out fear, because fear involves torment." Fear can bring demonic oppression.

Unforgiveness. Jesus said in Matthew 18 that people who don't forgive will be given over to the tormentors. In the parable of the unforgiving servant we read about a man who would not forgive. Jesus tells the whole story and then says, "So My heavenly Father also will do to you if each of you, from his heart, does not forgive his brother his trespasses" (v. 35). Verse 34 says, "And his master was angry, and delivered him to the torturers until he should pay all that was due to him." Forgiveness is a key to deliverance; in fact, forgiveness *brings* deliverance.

Accursed objects. Joshua 6:18 tells us, "By all means abstain from the accursed things, lest you become accursed when you take of the accursed things, and make the camp of Israel a curse, and trouble it." If you bring something that is cursed into your home, you will be cursed too. This is very important. Curses can be brought into your home by demonic images, artwork, statues, tribal masks, and other accursed objects. Please take this seriously.

Marks on the body. Now, I'm going to hit on something that people are not going to like, but I have to be faithful to teach you from the Word. Tattoos and body piercings are forbidden in the Word, as they can be an open door to bondage. Leviticus 19:28, Leviticus 21:4–5, Deuteronomy 14:1, and Jeremiah 16:6 all forbid Christians from having marks on their bodies. There are even more scriptures that forbid us to allow these things on our bodies because they attract demons.

Demons are attracted by sight, sound, and smell. Let me say that again: demons are attracted by things they see, things they hear, and things they smell. And what do you find in cults today? Images, drumbeats, and incense. What do you find in false religions? Those same three things: images they worship; drumbeats, chants, or sounds they repeat; and incense they burn. Demons are attracted to that stuff.

Be very careful of what you allow in that regard. When people put marks on their bodies, it is a pagan practice. As long as you did it before salvation, God forgives and forgets. But once you are saved, you know what the Bible says: not allowed.

When You Repent, Things Happen

True repentance is one of the greatest keys to freedom. When you repent, things happen. You don't have to go to someone else to cast out the devil. You can literally have self-deliverance through repentance. The Lord says if you don't forgive, you will be tormented. Beloved, we have to repent. And the Bible is clear on repentance: it is the quickest way out of bondage. I have seen this in my own life and in the lives of others.

Second Timothy 2:25–26 says, "In humility correcting those who are in opposition, if God perhaps will grant them repentance, so that they may know the truth, and that they may come to their senses and escape the snare of the devil, having been taken captive by him to do his will." How do they recover themselves from the snare of the devil? By renouncing and confessing. Repentance means you renounce something, you forsake it, you confess it, and you walk away from it, because confession by itself is not enough. "Whoso confesseth and forsaketh [his sins] shall have mercy," we are told in Proverbs 28:13 (KJV).

Years ago, I didn't know what I know today. I remember once during the '70s I was on my way to minister at a service in the Holy Land when I suddenly felt heavy oppression. I thought, "What is going on with me?" I was on a bus with a group of people, and I asked the Lord to forgive me for holding an offense against someone because I knew that whatever was coming against me mentally was not of the Lord. As I sat on that bus, I began talking to the Lord, repenting and asking for forgiveness. I was instantly delivered on the bus. Just like that, I was free and went right into the service.

But I had to repent. I was very specific with God about what happened. Sometimes you say things you shouldn't say or look at things you shouldn't look at, and the next thing you know, *wham*, it hits you right in the head. You can feel the oppression. It happens to all of us; it's happened to me more than once. But you learn through these experiences. You learn to *not allow these things*.

When people hurt us, we can go after them and hurt them or refuse to forgive them, but we will pay the price through torment. Forgiveness is a great liberator from oppression. I learned that painfully, the hard way.

Sometimes it's not easy to forgive—you want to go after the person and make them feel it. But no. Forgiving others is a quick way to prevent things happening that you don't want to happen. Trust me. This is what Paul was talking about in 2 Timothy 2 when he said acknowledging the truth will bring deliverance. Go back to the Word of God and do what God says.

Deliverance comes when we pray. Isaiah 52:2 tells us:

> Shake yourself from the dust, arise; sit down, O Jerusalem! Loose yourself from the bonds of your neck, O captive daughter of Zion!

That's deliverance. But how? Verse 1 tells us: deliverance came when they woke up.

> Awake, awake! Put on your strength, O Zion; put on your beautiful garments, O Jerusalem, the holy city! For the uncircumcised and the unclean shall no longer come to you.
> —Isaiah 52:1

What does it mean to *awake*? It means when you pray, you can shake yourself from the dust, arise, and sit down—you are now a threat to the powers of hell. You are free from that bondage. It's time to get free, beloved. No more bondage!

A COVENANT TO KEEP

1. In Jesus Christ you have the authority to crush Satan. Read Romans 16:20, and in your own words, describe what it says on the lines below.

_____

_____

2. Satan wants no part of worshipping God. He rebelled against the presence and worship of God. So as you worship God, he flees. As you enter the throne room of the Father through the shed blood of Jesus, Satan is powerless to touch, attack, harass, or accuse you.

   Here are some practical steps you can take to boldly approach the Father's throne through the blood:

   - Pray boldly.

   - Pray in the Spirit.

   - Sing praises to the Lord and play praise music.

   - Shout unto God with the voice of triumph.

   - Apply the blood of Jesus to every person and circumstance in your life.

   - Serve and minister unto the Lord by serving others in His name.

Heavenly Father, help me to keep Your Word ever before my eyes, written on the tablet of my heart, and alive within me. Thank You that because of Jesus' blood I no longer belong to the devil but to You. In the name of Your Son I pray. Amen.

Chapter 18

The GREAT SEAL

SEVERAL YEARS AGO, I had the privilege to meet and visit with Pope John Paul II. As the recognized head of the Roman Catholic Church, the pope wears a ring that is a symbol of his position in the church. It hearkens back to a time when those in the highest places of authority sealed their official documents and decrees with a mark from their ring. The ring was only a symbol of the power and authority behind it. Yet when an official seal of this nature appeared on a document, it communicated the same degree of power as if the authority figure issuing a decree was literally present.

This is true when we speak of the blood. As my dear friend Maxwell Whyte said, "It is not enough to believe in an historic blood of Calvary. It is necessary that we believe in the fountain NOW, and by faith avail ourselves of its power and life. Love is only a word until it is demonstrated; and in like manner, Blood is only a word until it is used. Ammunition in an arsenal is useless. It must be taken and *used* to bring terror to the enemy. The army of the Lord is powerless until it uses its weapons; these weapons are mighty to the bringing down of strongholds (2 Cor. 10:4). They are the Sword of the Spirit, which is the Word of God, and the Blood, for we read in Revelation 12:11, 'They overcame [Satan] by the blood of the Lamb and by the word of their testimony.' We need the WORD and the BLOOD."[1]

When we are washed by His blood and cleansed by the Word, the Bible tells us that the Lord places the seal of the Holy Spirit on us. That seal is a representation of the power behind it. Paul wrote:

> In Him you also trusted, after you heard the word of truth, the gospel of your salvation; in whom also, having believed, you were sealed with the Holy Spirit of promise, who is the guarantee of our inheritance until the redemption of the purchased possession, to the praise of His glory.
>
> —EPHESIANS 1:13–14

This seal is a symbol of protection. It says, "This is Mine. Put it aside, and leave it for Me. No one is to touch it because I am coming back to claim it."

The Lord does not seal anything that He does not plan to redeem. And He would not build mansions, as the Word of God declares, unless He was waiting for us to come home. (See John 14:2–3.)

We will remain sealed until Christ takes us home "to an inheritance incorruptible and undefiled and that does not fade away, reserved in heaven for you" (1 Pet. 1:4).

The inheritance is for those "who are kept by the power of God through faith for salvation ready to be revealed in the last time" (1 Pet. 1:5).

The seal will not be removed until His final work has been completed. Paul said that we "who have the firstfruits of the Spirit, even we ourselves groan within ourselves, eagerly waiting for the adoption, the redemption of our body" (Rom. 8:23).

The work is complete when the final trumpet sounds.

> The dead will be raised incorruptible, and we shall be changed. For this corruptible must put on incorruption, and this mortal must put on immortality. So when this corruptible has put on incorruption, and this mortal has put on immortality, then shall be brought to pass the saying that is written: "Death is swallowed up in victory."
>
> —1 CORINTHIANS 15:52–54

SEVENTY TIMES SEVEN

As long as you accept by faith what Christ's blood has done for you, no power on earth can break God's seal (2 Tim. 1:12).

> For I am persuaded that neither death nor life, nor angels nor principalities nor powers, nor things present nor things to come, nor height nor depth, nor any other created thing, shall be able to separate us from the love of God which is in Christ Jesus our Lord.
>
> —ROMANS 8:38–39

You may ask, "Are you telling me that God loves me in spite of myself?"

Yes. Regardless of our inconsistencies, He still loves us. He adopted us even though we were responsible for the death of His Son. And He welcomes us back even when we falter and fail.

Some people worry, "What if I make the same mistake again and again? Will He still pardon me?"

Peter asked Jesus the same question.

> "Lord, how often shall my brother sin against me, and I forgive him? Up to seven times?" Jesus said to him, "I do not say to you, up to seven times, but up to seventy times seven."
>
> —MATTHEW 18:21–22

The Lord's answer does not mean Christians can live in sin without repenting and still make heaven. Far from it. Those who abuse the forgiving nature of God have never experienced His true salvation. What God offers is more than eternal security—He gives us eternal grace.

It is God's transforming grace that makes redemption possible and prepares us to live godly lives.

> For the grace of God that brings salvation has appeared to all men, teaching us that, denying ungodliness and worldly lusts,

we should live soberly, righteously, and godly in the present age, looking for the blessed hope and glorious appearing of our great God and Savior Jesus Christ, who gave Himself for us, that He might redeem us from every lawless deed and purify for Himself His own special people, zealous for good works.

—TITUS 2:11–14

When you come face to face with the saving grace of God, it will bring a hunger for righteousness and godliness.

Because of the finished work of Calvary, God sent His Holy Spirit to provide us with strength to live holy lives. Paul said that we "do not live according to the flesh but according to the Spirit" (Rom. 8:4, NIV).

What God said to the prophet Zechariah is still true:

"Not by might nor by power, but by My Spirit," says the LORD of hosts. "Who are you, O great mountain? Before Zerubbabel you shall become a plain! And he shall bring forth the capstone with shouts of 'Grace, grace to it!'"

—ZECHARIAH 4:6–7

You may be facing temptation that seems like a mountain that will crush you. But because of the Spirit of the Lord and because of His grace, you can destroy that mountain and tear it apart stone by stone.

THE POWER OF GRACE

With God's grace comes great power.

With great power the apostles gave witness to the resurrection of the Lord Jesus. And great grace was upon them all.

—ACTS 4:33

In the Book of Acts we see what the power of God accomplished in the first Christians.

They received power and became witnesses.

"But you shall receive power when the Holy Spirit has come upon you; and you shall be witnesses to Me" (Acts 1:8).

The Holy Spirit changed their speech.

They began speaking in unknown tongues (Acts 2:4) and speaking God's Word with boldness (Acts 4:31).

Their demeanor was changed.

Stephen was the most dramatic example of this. When the Holy Spirit came upon Stephen while he was on trial, "all who sat in the council, looking steadfastly at him, saw his face as the face of an angel" (Acts 6:15). I believe that when God's anointing is on someone, the presence of the Holy Spirit is evident to those around that person. There is a look of divine power and joy on his or her face, a sense of authority in the person's voice. That's why Peter and John told the lame man, "Look at us" (Acts 3:4). When that lame man looked at them, they knew he would be able to see that the power of God was upon them.

One of the things I will never forget about Kathryn Kuhlman is that every time the anointing came on her, her eyes would change. They would have a sparkle in them.

I've noticed something over the years. Anytime the anointing leaves a servant of God, the sparkle goes; the fire goes. I recall a man who came to visit my church. At one time he was one of the mightiest men of God in Canada. But when I looked at him, there was no sparkle, no fire anymore. The anointing was gone, and his countenance showed it.

The Holy Spirit gave them boldness.

"Now when they saw the boldness of Peter and John, and perceived that they were uneducated and untrained men, they marveled" (Acts 4:13). They had no more fear but glorious boldness to proclaim the good news of the gospel.

The Holy Spirit changed their relationships.

Peter said that he was a witness of what Jesus had done "and so also is the Holy Spirit" (Acts 5:32). Here we see the Holy Spirit as their companion and helper.

The Holy Spirit changed their position.

Stephen began as an usher in the church (Acts 6:5), but he ended up being a mighty evangelist (Acts 6:8–10).

The Holy Spirit changed their vision.

"But he, being full of the Holy Spirit, gazed into heaven and saw the glory of God, and Jesus standing at the right hand of God" (Acts 7:55).

The Holy Spirit's great power is available to us today because we have also received God's "great grace."

The Holy Spirit in our lives is a reminder that Christ has bled and died, risen again, and ascended to the right hand of His Father. Jesus Himself asked His disciples to remember Him in another special way. My eyes were opened to a rich, new meaning in this remembrance by a group of Charismatic nuns.

A COVENANT TO KEEP

A seal is a symbol of protection. The Lord does not seal anything that He does not plan to redeem. And He would not build mansions unless He was waiting for us to come home (John 14:2–3). We will remain sealed until Christ takes us home "to an inheritance incorruptible and undefiled and that does not fade away, reserved in heaven for you" (1 Pet. 1:4). The inheritance is for those "who are kept by the power of God through faith for salvation ready to be revealed in the last time" (1 Pet. 1:5).

1. Scripture reveals many things about our eternal inheritance. Look up the promises listed on the chart about your inheritance and describe each one.

Bible Promise	My inheritance is . . .
Psalm 16:5	
Psalm 37:18	
Ephesians 1:11–14	
Ephesians 1:18–19	
Colossians 1:13–15	
Hebrews 9:15	
I Peter 1:3–5	

2. The Holy Spirit has sealed you for an eternal inheritance through the shed blood of Jesus Christ. Whom do you know that needs to be sealed by His Spirit? On the lines below, write the name of each person for whom you will begin praying who needs to confess Jesus as Lord and Savior and be sealed by His Spirit.

Now pray for each of these persons by name. You may wish to pray these words:

Lord Jesus, I pray for [insert the names], that Your precious Holy Spirit would convict them and lead them to repentance and salvation through Your blood that they might be sealed unto Your eternal inheritance. Amen.

3. It is God's transforming grace that makes redemption possible and prepares us to live godly lives. "For the grace of God that brings salvation has appeared to all men, teaching us that, denying ungodliness and worldly lusts, we should live soberly, righteously, and godly in the present age, looking for the blessed hope and glorious appearing of our great God and Savior Jesus Christ, who gave Himself for us, that He might redeem us from every lawless deed and purify for Himself His own special people, zealous for good works" (Titus 2:11–14).

How would you define grace?

Precious Jesus, thank You for shedding Your blood, which cleanses me and protects me. I am protected under its seal until You come to take us home. Father, thank You for forgiving me even when I fail. Your love knows no bounds. Amen.

Chapter 19

The COMMUNION in the COMMUNION

S EVERAL YEARS AGO I held a crusade where more than twelve thousand people jammed a coliseum at a fairgrounds to hear the Word of God preached.

As I ministered on the platform, my eyes were drawn to a group of Roman Catholic nuns dressed in distinctive ankle-length habits. They were seated near the front in the massive crowd.

Because I was taught by Catholic nuns in my school when I was a boy, I have a special place in my heart for them. At one point in the service I called them up onto the platform—forty-nine in all. We talked, and I discovered they were Catholic Charismatics who had driven six hours to attend the service.

Before they returned to their seats, I invited the nuns to join me in leading the people in a verse of "How Great Thou Art." As we sang the familiar lyrics, the expressions on their faces were almost angelic. It was evident that they loved the Lord deeply. Just before the closing line of the song, the Catholic nuns standing with me on the platform did something I will never forget. With spontaneous choreographed perfection, each one of the forty-nine Catholic nuns produced a wooden cross from her habit and raised it heavenward. They all sang the final chorus, "How great Thou art, how great Thou art!" It was a very powerful moment in the service. The crowd of twelve-thousand strong who sang with the Catholic nuns in unison was moved by this demonstration of surrender and worship.

After the service I had a little more time to talk with the nuns. I learned they belonged to an order that was founded by their mother general, a tall woman with piercing blue eyes. (I found out later

193

that a mother general is even higher in authority than a mother superior.)

"Why don't you come and visit our convent?" the mother general asked me.

"I would love to come," I told her.

A few months later I accepted the invitation. The convent was located on rolling hills in a river valley. The sisters built all of the buildings themselves, including a retreat center and a farm where they raise their own food.

The sisters served me and a few friends who had accompanied me a beautiful turkey dinner, complete with vegetables they had grown themselves.

After dinner they asked, "Would you mind if we served you Communion?"

"Not at all. I would love it," I said. (Apparently, they felt it would be permissible to serve me because I had been baptized in the Greek Orthodox Church as a child.)

I didn't realize the Lord had something special in store for me that night that would impact my life greatly.

All forty-nine nuns, along with my friends and me, went to the newly built prayer chapel. The nuns began worshipping the Lord, singing in the Spirit and blessing the Lord for about half an hour.

The sisters gave several words of prophecy that encouraged me. By then I was on my knees crying because I sensed such a tremendous presence of the Lord there.

It was an anointing I had never before experienced in a Communion service, not even in my own church. There was a divine, powerful presence of God that I can't describe except to say Jesus walked into that little room.

Just as they were finishing that time of worship, I began to feel a numbness in my arms and chest. I didn't know that the mother general had just gone to the table and picked up the Communion wafer. Now she began to speak the words of the apostle Paul from 1 Corinthians 11:23:

194

> For I received from the Lord that which I also delivered to
> you: that the Lord Jesus on the same night in which He was
> betrayed took bread.

As I was kneeling and praising the Lord with my hands extended directly in front of me, the mother general put the wafer in my mouth.

At that moment I felt a fire go through me, and as that took place something else amazing happened. I sensed on the tips of my fingers something like a robe—a soft, silky fabric.

I thought maybe I was touching one of the sisters' robes or that my mind was playing tricks on me. I wasn't sure what it was, so I opened my eyes to see whether someone had stepped in front of me. There was no one.

I wanted to make sure it wasn't just my imagination, so I closed my eyes again. By this time, I was weeping and basking in God's presence that filled the room. Again I felt the robe. I thought, "This can't be." I opened my eyes again. As before, nothing was there.

I closed my eyes a third time, and as quickly as I did, I felt the same thing again—some type of soft, flowing fabric. I paused for a moment, and I moved my hands closer toward each other. Then I was stopped, for I could not move them any closer. Something was there in front of me. I felt what seemed like a person's body. It's difficult to describe and even harder to understand.

The experience I had that evening as I knelt there in prayer was unlike anything I had ever known. It was glorious and indescribable. It was as if I was kneeling at the feet of Jesus.

After that Communion service, I couldn't quit singing. That entire night I felt as if I were floating. I went back to my hotel room and asked the Lord, "What happened to me?" The Lord opened my understanding about the subject of Communion.

Whenever we partake of Communion, we are having communion with the Lord. When we celebrate the Lord's Supper, He is there.

I want to share with you what the Lord showed me through that experience and what I learned as I studied the Word. In 1 Corinthians 10:16 the Bible says:

> The cup of blessing which we bless, is it not the communion of the blood of Christ? The bread which we break, is it not the communion of the body of Christ?

This verse says, "There is communion in the Communion." Often when we take Communion, we don't realize that we are to have communion with the Lord Himself. It's not just a practice because of tradition or what we were told by our fathers or mothers. Yes, it's a remembrance of what Jesus did for us two thousand years ago at Calvary. But at the same time, it is a communion with Him in the present! He comes today to fellowship with you just as your son or daughter or loved one would.

Even though I'd been a Christian and a preacher for many years, it was not until that night at the convent that I began to see something new in the Communion. The fact is, when we have Communion, Jesus wants to come and have fellowship with us as we partake of "the Lord's Supper."

We call it the Lord's Supper because it's His supper, not ours.

Of course, I don't mean to suggest that people ought to expect to have the same experience I had. I believe the Lord revealed Himself to me that evening in that unusual way in order to teach me. Yet Communion is always a time when the presence of the Lord can be very real to our spiritual senses.

BEING WORTHY

I was so thrilled by this new understanding about the Lord's Supper that I wanted to do everything I could to keep the "communion in the Communion." Paul's warning in the Scriptures became so real:

> Therefore whoever eats this bread or drinks this cup of the
> Lord in an unworthy manner will be guilty of the body and
> blood of the Lord.
>
> —1 CORINTHIANS 11:27

Why was he saying this to the Corinthian church? What would cause them to turn Communion into a vain ceremony? The apostle Paul gives us five reasons:

1. There were divisions among them. "For first of all, when ye come together in the church, I hear that there be divisions among you; and I partly believe it" (1 Cor. 11:18, KJV).

2. There were heretical teachings in the church. "For there must be also heresies among you, that they which are approved may be made manifest among you" (1 Cor. 11:19, KJV).

3. We see selfishness in this church. "For in eating every one taketh before other his own supper: and one is hungry, and another is drunken" (1 Cor. 11:21, KJV).

4. They despised the house of God. "What? have ye not houses to eat and to drink in? or despise ye the church of God...?" (1 Cor. 11:22, KJV).

5. They had become very proud and looked down on others. "...and shame them that have not?" (1 Cor. 11:22, KJV).

When Paul warned against celebrating the Lord's Supper in an unworthy manner, he was talking about the sins in the Corinthian church. Some of their sins were even committed at the Lord's table!

Paul said that many of the Corinthians were "weak and sick," and some had even died because of their lack of discernment. That's a negative thing. But by the same token, if we partake worthily, I believe there will be health and strength rather than weakness and sickness. Paul goes on to say:

> For if we would judge ourselves, we would not be judged. But when we are judged, we are chastened by the Lord, that we may not be condemned with the world.
>
> —1 CORINTHIANS 11:31–32

If we would judge ourselves, then God wouldn't have to judge us. But if He does judge, He is only doing it for the sake of your redemption. In Psalm 32 we see both kinds of judgment—how God judges man and how man can judge himself.

Listen to the way David describes himself when he "kept silent"—in other words, when he did not judge himself and confess his sin.

> When I kept silent, my bones grew old through my groaning all the day long.
>
> —PSALM 32:3

Here we see that when he didn't confess his sin, his physical body was affected. Remember that Paul said, "For this reason [participating in Communion unworthily] many are weak and sick among you" (1 Cor. 11:30).

God often judges us by withdrawing a sense of His presence from us. Living without the presence of the Lord is like the dryness of a summer without rain.

> For day and night thy hand was heavy upon me: my moisture is turned into the drought of summer.
>
> —PSALM 32:4, KJV

So how can we come back into the Lord's favor? David demonstrates what to do.

I acknowledged my sin to You, and my iniquity I have not hidden. I said, "I will confess my transgressions to the LORD," and You forgave the iniquity of my sin.

—PSALM 32:5

Speaking of David, the Lord said, "He is a man after My own heart." (See 1 Samuel 13:14.) Why? Because David sought after the Lord.

When the prophet Samuel told Saul that God had rejected him, Saul asked Samuel for forgiveness (1 Sam. 15:25). When the prophet Nathan confronted David for stealing another man's wife, you don't find David saying, "Forgive me, Nathan." (See 2 Samuel 12.) Rather he said, "Have mercy upon me, O God" (Ps. 51:1).

The big difference between David and Saul was this: Saul sought forgiveness; David sought the One who forgives.

David sought God and asked Him to forgive him. We also must confess our sins to the Lord. The Bible says when we acknowledge our transgressions to Him, "You forgave the iniquity of my sin" (Ps. 32:5).

Amazingly, the Bible calls those who confess their sins godly.

For this cause everyone who is godly shall pray to You in a time when You may be found.

—PSALM 32:6

Look at how David's relationship with God changed after he confessed his sin. He wrote:

You are my hiding place; You shall preserve me from trouble; You shall surround me with songs of deliverance.

—PSALM 32:7

So we see the way God responds when we repent.

Paul states that we must judge ourselves before partaking of the Lord's Supper. How do we judge ourselves? By confessing our sins.

And what is the result? Communion with the Lord is restored.

WHAT DO WE REMEMBER?

When Jesus was celebrating the first Communion with His disciples, He told them, "Do this in remembrance of Me" (Luke 22:19). What should we remember when we come to the Lord's table?

First, dear saint, I know you thank God that Jesus died in your place to free you from the consequences of your sins. But He did so many other things for you on the cross.

The Bible declares that Jesus suffered rejection and became acquainted with grief for you and me.

> He is despised and rejected by men, a Man of sorrows and acquainted with grief.
>
> —ISAIAH 53:3

On the cross Jesus bore our sins and the consequences of our sins.

> Surely He has borne our griefs and carried our sorrows.
>
> —ISAIAH 53:4

The word *grief* here is the Hebrew *choliy*, which means weak, sick, or afflicted. Surely He has borne our weaknesses, sicknesses, and afflictions. The Hebrew word for *sorrows* is *makob*, which means "pain" or "grief."

The Scriptures are clear: Jesus not only died to take away our sins; He also died to take away our sicknesses. The New Testament confirms that fact in Matthew 8:16–17:

> When evening had come, they brought to Him many who were demon-possessed. And He cast out the spirits with a word, and healed all who were sick, that it might be fulfilled which was spoken by Isaiah the prophet, saying: "He Himself took our infirmities and bore our sicknesses."

Matthew was referring to Isaiah 53:4, which speaks of Christ being stricken, smitten, and afflicted. So Jesus died not only to take away your sins but also to take away your sicknesses.

I believe the psalmist was speaking prophetically of the benefits of the cross when he wrote Psalm 103.

> Bless the LORD, O my soul, and forget not all His benefits.
>
> —PSALM 103:2

Why shouldn't we forget His benefits? I believe when you forget what God has done for you, He is grieved. The psalmist said of the children of Israel:

> Again and again they tempted God, and pained the Holy One of Israel. They did not remember His power, the day when He redeemed them from the adversary.
>
> —PSALM 78:41–42, NASB

It's important to God that you remember what He has done for you. That's why we celebrate the Lord's Supper—to remember all the good things He has done for us through the cross. As we look at these benefits found in Psalm 103, please notice that they are all present tense. They are available to you today.

- "Who forgives all your iniquities" (v. 3). All your sins are washed; all your sins are forgiven. All you have to do is repent and receive Him as your Savior.

- "Who heals all your diseases" (v. 3). I'm so glad the verse doesn't say, "Who forgave" and "who healed." It says, "Who forgives"—present tense—and "who heals"—present tense. He still forgives; He still heals.

- "Who redeems your life from destruction" (v. 4).

- "Who crowns you with lovingkindness and tender mercies" (v. 4).

- "Who satisfies your mouth with good things" (v. 5). The Bible says God satisfies you with good things. He never gives bad things; He always gives good things. As my friend Oral Roberts said, "God is a good God."

- "So that your youth is renewed like the eagle's" (v. 5). When we know His benefits, He'll renew us.

- "The LORD executes righteousness and justice for all who are oppressed" (v. 6). Because of the cross, we are defended from the oppressor.

I want to share with you one more benefit of the cross that the Lord showed me many years ago. It has blessed me greatly.

COME INTO THE THRONE ROOM

Paul tells us in Philippians 2:5–8 something wonderful about what Jesus has done for us. He took seven "steps" to descend from His heavenly throne to the cross.

1. "Who, being in the form of God, did not consider it robbery to be equal with God" (v. 6)

2. "But made Himself of no reputation" (v. 7)

3. "Taking the form of a bondservant" (v. 7)

4. "And coming in the likeness of men" (v. 7)

5. "And being found in appearance as a man" (v. 8)

6. "He humbled Himself" (v. 8)

7. "And became obedient to the point of death, even the death of the cross" (v. 8)

And, as we read in Philippians 2:9–11, God took seven "steps" to restore His throne to Him.

1. "Therefore God also has highly exalted Him" (v. 9)

2. "And given Him the name which is above every name" (v. 9)

3. "That at the name of Jesus every knee should bow" (v. 10)

4. "Of those in heaven" (v. 10)

5. "And of those on earth" (v. 10)

6. "And of those under the earth" (v. 10)

7. "And that every tongue should confess that Jesus Christ is Lord, to the glory of God the Father" (v. 11)

In the Book of Hebrews, Scripture declares that after the Lord Jesus purged our sins, He "sat down at the right hand of the Majesty on high" (Heb. 1:3). Sitting speaks symbolically of a finished work; the right hand speaks of power. Jesus received all authority and all power. "Majesty on high" speaks of His being the King of kings and Lord of lords.

Because the Lord is on that throne, the Bible says we have "boldness to enter the Holiest by the blood of Jesus" (Heb. 10:19). Jesus went from the *throne to the cross* to save us. He went from the *cross to the throne* to become our High Priest and enable us to enter God's presence.

Whenever you celebrate the Lord's Supper, remember that it is because of the blood of Jesus Christ that we can have fellowship with God. And as we recall what He has done for us when His body was broken and His blood was shed, then the presence of God will descend.

I've seen in my own experience that through the blood of Jesus, the anointing of God always comes—not only on my private, personal prayer life but even during the great miracle services.

I never conduct a service without thanking the Lord for the blood.

For I have discovered that where the blood is honored, the presence of God descends and miracles take place. In the Old Covenant, God responded with fire when blood was offered on the altar. So it is today. When the blood of Jesus is honored, when the work of the cross is honored, the Holy Spirit comes and touches people's lives.

It is my prayer that the presence of the Holy Spirit will increase and become great in your life as a result of reading this book. I pray your love for the Lord will be enlarged until that glorious day when you shall see Him face to face.

A Covenant to Keep

1. In 1 Corinthians 10:16, the Bible says, "The cup of blessing which we bless, is it not the communion of the blood of Christ? The bread which we break, is it not the communion of the body of Christ?" This verse says, "There is communion in the Communion." Often when we take Communion, we don't realize that we are to have communion with the Lord Himself.

   Each of the following verses tells us something about the Lord's Supper. Read each of the verses and describe what that verse says to you about your communion with the living Christ.

Matthew 26:26–29

_____

_____

Luke 22:14–22

_____

_____

John 6:53–58

_____

_____

1 Corinthians 10:16–17

_____

_____

2. Isaiah 53 speaks prophetically of many of the things that Jesus' death on the cross would accomplish in the life of the believer. Read this chapter. On the lines below, describe the benefits Isaiah listed as a result of Jesus' sacrifice.

_____

_____

3. In Philippians 2:5–8, Paul shares the seven "steps" Jesus took to descend from His heavenly throne to the cross. As I share with you these seven steps, consider your own walk with God. How can these steps become real in your daily life? Answer the question after the description of each step.

"Who, being in the form of God, did not consider it robbery to be equal with God" (v. 6). What daily action can you take to avoid "playing God" in your own life?

_____

_____

"But made Himself of no reputation" (v. 7). Describe the reputation you have as a follower of Jesus Christ.

_____

_____

"Taking the form of a bondservant" (v. 7). How will you be a servant to Jesus?

_____

_____

"And coming in the likeness of men" (v. 7). How are you being transformed into His likeness?

_____

_____

"And being found in appearance as a man" (v. 8). How does the Holy Spirit manifest Himself in you?

_____

_____

"He humbled Himself" (v. 8). In what or whom do you take pride?

_____

_____

"And became obedient to the point of death, even the death of the cross" (v. 8). Under what circumstances would you die for Jesus?

_____

_____

Jesus, thank You that because of Your sacrifice, I can enjoy fellowship with the Father today. Broken and spilled out, You died for my sins so that we may be joined together forever. Holy Spirit, every time that I partake of Communion—whether privately or corporately—help me to always be mindful of the significance and the value in it. May I never take Communion for granted, in Jesus' name. Amen.

Appendix

PLEADING the
BLOOD for
HOUSEHOLD SALVATION

I WAS PLEASANTLY SURPRISED during a worship service several years ago to look out and see the familiar face of a young man sitting in the congregation. I invited him to join us on the platform, and as the anointing of the Holy Spirit fell upon him moments later, we were all deeply moved. Brushing away my own tears, I reflected back to a much more difficult time in this young man's life.

Our dear friends, his parents, were near their wits' end with him. Although they loved the Lord and served Him in ministry, both of their teenage children were living in angry rebellion toward God. Suzanne and I had attempted to counsel both the son and the daughter on more than one occasion, but the two young people just sat like frozen statues before us. We never broke through that wall of rebellion.

Finally, feeling a little frustrated with their stubbornness, I said, "Look, you can't escape. Your mother and daddy are praying for you." Still, their expressions remained frozen in bitter silence.

Several years later, however, the scene changed. Now young adults, they were both serving the Lord joyfully, with all of their hearts. Both were involved in powerful, anointed ministries. As their parents discussed the transformation with us, their mother mentioned something that deeply stirred my spirit. She said, "When we prayed and asked the Lord to save our children, He said, 'I am a covenant-keeping God.'"

God revealed to her a key He had shown me in my own life as a young man during a season in which I battled in prayer for the souls of my own family members. What God revealed was this: Salvation is a covenant that extends beyond an individual believer to include his or her entire family. If you have a loved one who is not saved, I want you to know that God is a covenant-keeping God. Because of the covenant of salvation, a blood covenant made with Christ's own blood, you have great authority to pray for your loved ones to be saved.

A LAMB FOR A HOUSEHOLD

In Exodus 12:3, God commanded Moses to take a lamb for a house. "Speak ye unto all the congregation of Israel, saying, In the tenth day of this month they shall take to them every man a lamb, according to the house of their fathers, a lamb for an house" (KJV).

The lamb was offered during the Feast of Passover for the forgiveness of sins. During the Passover Feast, every Hebrew household would offer one lamb for their entire family—a lamb for a house. God revealed a powerful truth through this word picture. When one person received the lamb, it became available for his or her entire family. Today, Christ is our Passover Lamb, slain for our redemption. His precious blood was poured out to seal that covenant for you and me.

Your place in God gives you a special position of intercessory prayer for your family's salvation. Remember, the Lord didn't say a lamb for a person. He said a lamb for a house. When you received salvation, a door of special grace was opened to them too.

Throughout the Bible we see many examples of one righteous person interceding for the salvation of his or her entire family. Noah's entire family was delivered because of his relationship with God. Abraham and Lot are another example. Lot lived in Sodom, but because of Abraham's intercessory prayers for his nephew, he was saved from death when the city was destroyed.

Even in the New Testament, when Paul and Silas were imprisoned for their faith, they spoke God's promise to the jailer. They said, "Believe on the Lord Jesus Christ, and you will be saved, you and your household" (Acts 16:31).

TAKING YOUR PLACE

The power of covenant in which we live is based upon the blood of Christ. Learning to take your place as intercessor for your family, as Abraham did for Lot, requires that you understand how the power of the blood of Christ affects your prayers.

Appropriating the blood of Christ as we pray is extremely important. Each time you say "I plead the blood" in prayer, you are actually saying, "I recognize and appropriate the power represented in the blood, and I remind the enemy of his defeat because of that blood."

Some say that pleading the blood over our families as we pray for their salvation is like begging Satan to leave them alone. Although I don't doubt their sincerity, they couldn't be more mistaken. You see, pleading the blood is not begging. Rather, it's much like entering a plea in court.

The accuser, Satan, stands before God, the Judge of the entire universe, and he points to your loved one, lists his or her sins, and demands eternal damnation. Sadly, the accuser is right. Your loved one stands completely condemned based upon his or her sin. The Bible says, "All have sinned and fall short of the glory of God" (Rom. 3:23). That means that no matter how good your loved one has been, he or she has certainly sinned. Again, the Bible says, "There is none who does good, no, not one" (Rom. 3:12).

Your loved one stands completely condemned. He or she has sinned, and "the wages of sin is death" (Rom. 6:23). It seems hopeless.

But you, as an intercessor, can now come before the Judge and enter a plea. You say, "I realize my loved one is doomed because he or she has sinned. But I enter my plea: I plead the blood."

Suddenly everything in heaven's courtroom changes, for the blood represents Christ's death on behalf of your loved one. When Jesus Christ was born on earth, He was totally God and totally man. He became the only sinless human being. When He died, He could not be condemned, for He never sinned. Therefore, He was able to take your loved one's sins to the cross. (See 1 John 2:1.) On the cross, Christ became the Mediator—the Advocating Attorney—between God the righteous, perfect Judge and sinful humankind.

When you plead the blood for your loved one, you are not merely acknowledging your belief in the historic blood of Calvary. It is necessary that you believe and by faith avail yourself of its powers and life. When you say, "I plead the blood on behalf of my loved one," you do not contest the accusation of the devil. You say, "Yes. I realize that my loved one has sinned. However, I do not enter a guilty plea. My plea is 'The Blood.'"

By pointing to the blood of Christ, you are asking for mercy based upon the Lord's finished work on the cross. Christ paid the price for your loved one's guilt, shame, and failures.

Suddenly Satan the accuser backs off, for he remembers the power of his defeat at the cross.

Here's how heaven's court understands your plea. You are saying, "My loved one is guilty as charged. I do not contest the truth of his or her sinful past. Nevertheless, Christ paid the price of those sins. The guilty verdict fell on Him at the cross. Because of the blood of Christ, I ask that you release my loved one from the power of sin and the power of the devil's accusation against him or her."

As you appropriate the power of Christ's blood in the life of an individual, the power of sin and death that held him because of guilt is bound. The blood of Christ allows this individual the opportunity to choose salvation and new birth.

Now the resources of heaven are stirred on your loved one's behalf. The devil's power that held your loved one captive because of sin is pushed back. The chains that locked this person's heart and mind against the gospel begin to break as you continue to pray. Angels surround him or her. The Bible says, "Are they not all ministering spirits sent forth to minister for those who will inherit salvation?" (Heb. 1:14). God begins to move upon his or her heart to draw your loved one to salvation. The Word of God declares, "No one can come to Me unless the Father who sent Me draws him" (John 6:44).

As you continue to stand in prayer for your household, you can witness the salvation of each member. The Bible promises, "Receive the Lord and be saved, you and your house." (See Acts 16:31.)

Your intercession on behalf of your household is powerful when the blood of Christ is your plea against the accusations of the enemy that keep your loved ones bound to the power of sin.

When you plead the blood of Jesus Christ, you take the teeth out of the roaring lion. His only power to destroy you is based upon sin. When you plead the blood, that powerful grip is broken so that those who are held captive can become free.

APPROPRIATING THE BLOOD OF CHRIST

Praying for your loved ones' salvation is not the only powerful way that you can appropriate the blood of Jesus Christ. Healing, deliverance, protection, provision, overcoming a broken heart, and freedom from sin, guilt, and shame all come under its saving power. The finished work on the cross begins with salvation and flows to all of our other needs too.

When we appropriate the power of the blood during prayer, we are never using empty repetition. Rather, we boldly declare our understanding of the authority and power available to us through the finished work of the cross of Jesus Christ. When we plead the blood of Jesus Christ, we take the place of authority that He's given to us to overcome every need.

The blood of Christ has mighty power to save, heal, and deliver to the uttermost. There's power in the blood, healing in the blood, salvation in the blood, and deliverance in the mighty blood of Jesus!

Never forget that the blood of Christ represents the work of the cross, which is the source of all spiritual power.

Do you need healing? Deliverance? Salvation? Cleansing? Freedom from guilt and mental bondage? What about those you love? There's power in the blood of Jesus Christ for you right now!

A PRAYER FOR YOU

Here's a prayer that will help you begin to appropriate the power of Christ's blood for all of your needs and for the needs of your loved ones as well. Simply fill in the blanks and pray this prayer aloud from your heart.

Dear Lord,

I thank You for shedding Your precious blood on the cross for my salvation, healing, deliverance, cleansing, and wholeness. I am so grateful for Your wonderful love for me and for those whom I love. All I can say is a million thanks to You, dear Lord. What a wonderful Savior You are.

Today I come before You for _____, who needs Your touch. I plead the blood, Lord, and I am ever mindful that it's not our righteousness that saves, heals, and keeps us. For You alone are righteous, wonderful Lord. You alone are holy. I plead Your blood over _____'s life right now for _____ (healing, salvation, cleansing, deliverance, and/or help). Thank You for the price You paid for _____'s life. Thank You that _____ is so precious to You that You gave Your life for _____.

Because of the power of the blood of Jesus Christ, I declare that bondage is broken today in the mighty and precious name of Jesus.

And for the price You paid to save us, heal us, and deliver us, all we can say is a million thanks, Lord Jesus. Thank You that there's power in the blood!

NOTES

INTRODUCTION

1. Lewis E. Jones, "There Is Power in the Blood," public domain.
2. "O the Blood of Jesus," author unknown, public domain.
3. Phill McHugh, "Lamb of Glory," Shepherd's Fold Music (a div. of EMI Christian Publishing / River Oaks Music Company, a div. of EMI Christian Music Publishing), 1982. Used by permission.

CHAPTER 1

1. Maxwell Whyte, *The Power of the Blood* (Springdale, PA: Whitaker House, 1973), 87–88, 90.
2. Whyte, *The Power of the Blood*, 23.

CHAPTER 3

1. See comments on Genesis 3:21 from Jamieson, Fausset, and Brown and Adam Clarke in *The Bethany Parallel Commentary* (Minneapolis: Bethany House, 1985).
2. Henry M. Stanley, *Through the Dark Continent, Vol. 1* (New York: Dover Publications, 2013), 387.
3. H. Clay Trumbull, *The Blood Covenant* (Kirkwood, MO: Impact Books, 1975), 18–20.

CHAPTER 7

1. R. A. Torrey, *How to Obtain Fullness of Power* (Tarrytown, NY: Fleming H. Revell, 1897), 83.
2. Torrey, *How to Obtain Fullness of Power*, 83.
3. *The Best of E. M. Bounds on Prayer* (Grand Rapids, MI: Baker Book House, 1981), 27.

CHAPTER 8

1. David Alsobrook, *The Precious Blood* (Paducah, KY: David Alsobrook Ministries, 1977), 50–58.
2. *New Bible Dictionary*, ed. J. D. Douglas (Wheaton, IL: Tyndale House, 1987), s.v. "plants."

CHAPTER 9

1. Derek Prince, *The Spirit-Filled Believer's Handbook* (Lake Mary, FL: Charisma House, 1993), 251.
2. Andrew Murray, *The Power of the Blood* (Fort Washington, PA: Christian Literature Crusade, 1984), 28.

CHAPTER 10

1. Andrew Murray, *Absolute Surrender* (Fort Washington, PA: Christian Literature Crusade, 2000).
2. *The International Standard Bible Encyclopedia* (Grand Rapids, MI: Wm. B. Eerdmans, 1982), s.v. "shoe; sandal" by David M. Howard.

CHAPTER 11

1. Torrey, *How to Obtain Fullness of Power*, 33.
2. Torrey, *How to Obtain Fullness of Power*, 34.
3. Billy Graham, *Peace with God* (Nashville, TN: Thomas Nelson, 1984).
4. Whyte, *The Power of the Blood*, 21–22.
5. Jones, "There Is Power in the Blood."
6. Basilea Schlink, *Repentance: The Joy-Filled Life* (Minneapolis: Bethany House, 1984).

CHAPTER 12

1. Frederick Lehman, "The Love of God," public domain.
2. Murray, *The Power of the Blood*, 32–33.

CHAPTER 14

1. C. H. Spurgeon, "Honey From a Lion," No. 1591, sermon delivered on April 3, 1881, at the Metropolitan Tabernacle, Newington, London, accessed November 9, 2023, at Spurgeon's Sermons (V27), https://ccel.org/ccel/spurgeon/sermons27/sermons27.xvii.html.
2. Oswald Chambers, "October 28: Justification by Faith," in *My Utmost for His Highest* (Grand Rapids, MI: RBC Ministries, 1997).
3. Henry F. Lyte, "Praise, My Soul, the King of Heaven," adapted from Psalm 103, public domain.

CHAPTER 15

1. A. W. Tozer, *The Pursuit of God* (Harrisburg, PA: Christian Publications, 1948), 11.

CHAPTER 18

1. Whyte, *The Power of the Blood*, 58–59.

OTHER BOOKS
by BENNY HINN

Mysteries of the Anointing

Good Morning, Holy Spirit

Prayer That Gets Results

Welcome, Holy Spirit

Lamb of God

Blood in the Sand

The Biblical Road to Blessing

He Touched Me

The Miracle of Healing

FOR OTHER RESOURCES,
VISIT BENNY HINN MINISTRIES
AT BENNYHINN.ORG.